"Dr. Smith compels us to take a deep breath, bear down, and push past whatever it is that may be hindering us from giving birth to God's divine destiny for our lives."

-Dr. Cathy Owens-Oliver, Author & Speaker

"In Can I Push? Dr. Chevelta Smith encourages men and women to closely examine the process of birthing out a gift from God as she skillfully and joyfully compares the conception, prenatal care and delivery of a human child, to the conception, development and pushing forth of their purpose. In a striking and honest medical-spiritual comparison of this process, Dr. Smith reveals what it means when a believer is ready to birth or push out their God-given purpose, ministry, calling or mission."

–Ronald E. Davis, Freelance Editor & College Professor

"Dr. Chevelta Smith is a physician who was trained to help and heal women and bring lives into this world. Dr. Chevelta's real gift is healing all people with the Word of God. She truly is a gift from God who was sent here to heal our mind, body, and spirit!!"

–Dr. Kenneth Smith, Anesthesiologist & Medical Director

Can I Push?

Understanding the Process to Delivering Your Purpose

Dr. Chevelta A. Smith

Copyright © 2015 by Dr. Chevelta A. Smith.

All rights reserved. No part of this publication may be reproduced, distributed or transmitted in any form or by any means, including photocopying, recording, or other electronic or mechanical methods, without the prior written permission of the publisher, except in the case of brief quotations embodied in critical reviews and certain other noncommercial uses permitted by copyright law. For permission requests, write to the publisher, addressed "Attention: Permissions Coordinator," at the address below.

Dr. Chevelta A. Smith
info@rawmedicinelive.com

Front Cover Book Design: Sanya Nicole, LLC
Editors: Ronald E. Davis, Ivory S. Bostick, John H. Bostick

Ordering Information:
Quantity sales. Special discounts are available on quantity purchases by corporations, associations, and others. For details, contact the "Special Sales Department" at the address above.

Can I Push? Understanding the Process to Delivering Your Purpose/Dr. Chevelta A. Smith. —1st ed.
ISBN 978-0-578-16960-6

Dedication

To Greg, my husband, best friend, and lover.

After 23 years of marriage, you are still pushing me to be my best. For that I am grateful.

To Brookelynn, Morgan, and Caleb: my three amazing children. You each inspire me to be the best I can be. I pray my life will inspire you to keep pushing to be the best you can be and live your God-given purpose. I see greatness in each of you and can't wait for you to manifest it to the world.

Contents

Acknowledgments

Introduction

Chapter One	Are You Pregnant?	1
Chapter Two	The Release: *Ovulation*	14
Chapter Three	The Encounter: *Intercourse*	31
Chapter Four	The Deposit: *Fertilization And Conception*	51
Chapter Five	The Attachment: *Implantation*	65
Chapter Six	The Pregnancy: *Growth & Development*	77
Chapter Seven	The Labor Process	123
Chapter Eight	Time To Push	148
Chapter Nine	The Delivery	165
Chapter Ten	The Assessment: *Examination Of What Is Delivered*	176

About the Author

Acknowledgements

Thank God! I finally pushed out the greatness I believe I was born to manifest. I no longer wonder *What On Earth Am I Here For?* *(kudos to Rick Warren)*. Although this is my first book, it feels amazing to accomplish what I know I was created to do. Achieving my ultimate purpose is surreal and humbling; however, my ability to reach this point in my life is directly related to the tremendous love and support of my family and friends.

Family

To my parents, John and Ivory Bostick—from the time I was a little girl, you always believed in me. I thank you for teaching me to love God and the importance of making Him the center of my life. You have always taught me that, "I could do all things through Christ, who strengthens me!" I believed it then, and over four decades later, I still believe it and live it! You are absolutely the BEST parents in the world. Dad, thank you for your tremendous support and help with this book. Mom, thank you for being my greatest fan! Your listening ear, advice and encouragement throughout this book-writing process has been phenomenal. As the first author in our immediate family, you inspired me! You are such an amazing example of determination and drive. To my in-laws, John and Catherine Smith—thank you for your support and encouragement throughout this process. I felt your love from miles away.

To my Goddi, Sandra Jones—I am grateful to God for allowing you and my mom to become best friends over 25 years ago. In my eyes, you are and will always be my second mommy! Thank you for loving me like you've birthed me yourself. Your support while I wrote this book was more than I could ever imagine. Thank you for allowing me to call you at all times of the day (and night) to read portions of the book while I wrote. Your feedback and responses always gave me the push I needed to keep writing.

To my husband, Greg, daughters, Brookelynn and Mo, and son, Caleb—thank you so much for loving me and encouraging me throughout this process. Moreover, thank you for being patient and understanding the time needed to complete this assignment. Greg, you are my greatest supporter. You have always demonstrated your faith in me. What more could a woman ask for in a husband? Thank you for giving me the freedom to grow into the woman God designed me to be. Even more so, thank you for helping to mold me into who I am today. I am tremendously blessed to have you in my life. Your Men's Perspective contribution was awesome! It's one of my most favorite parts of the book! Thank you for your needed contribution to this project. Brookelynn and Mo, my queens in waiting. Your words of encouragement kept me strengthened throughout this assignment. To hear you say "Mami, I'm so proud of you!" means more than I could adequately express. Thank you for sharing your advice, perspectives, and opinions regarding my content and cover design. I valued both tremendously. I love the drive you two exhibit in your own lives, and honestly speaking, you two inspire me to go after my dreams. The mother-daughter bonds we have has made me feel like I can do anything! I am grateful to you both. Caleb, my prince. What can I say? You were my initial accountability partner. I am grateful that you kept me accountable to the task of writing. I enjoyed the times we would sit and write together. Thank you for all your writing tips! Moreover, thank you for your encouraging words! You amaze me!

To my sister, Shondale Gray—what can I say girl? Your creativity and suggestions have improved this book tremendously. I appreciate all of your editorial contributions to this work. You are awesome! You were divinely purposed to assist me right at the time you did. I would not have made it through the last leg of my process without you! Thank you and thanks to all "The Fam" for your love!

Colleagues

I am truly grateful to my colleague, Dr. Jewel Amui for taking the time to assist me in this journey. Your feedback and support was priceless. Dr. Annette Wagner, my OB/Gyn "Smith & Wesson" partner! You are my girl and my sister! Your support of this endeavor has meant so much to me. Thank you for being there. To Dr. Lucy Lot, and Peggy Boyd, CRNP—thank you so much for your feedback, encouragement, and support throughout this process. Peggy, your excitement kept me going at times I most needed it! We've got to write a book together. I can't wait!

Business

I especially want to thank Ronald E. Davis, who served as the chief editor for this book! He is amazing and great at what he does! His suggestions and feedback tremendously enhanced the manuscript. Additionally, I must thank my niece, Nicky Spencer, who designed my book cover and amazing Raw Medicine Logo! Your work and creativity is awesome! You captured it!

Friends

Dwight and Deidra Roussaw — Thank you so much for believing in everything I do. Your support and confidence in what God has placed inside of me is invaluable. Facebook family and friends, Ms. Charlene Day, Jamar Jones, Pastors Curtis and Vickie Jones of New Life and Spirit in Erie, Pa, Matt and Alexis Jones, my F.L.O.W. Center family, and all of you who spoke life to this project; everyone, thank you so much for the tremendous outpouring of support through encouraging words and prayers! Your excitement to receive the gift God allowed me to deliver is humbling!

Introduction

The doors of the Women & Children's department burst open, another laboring patient has arrived. This one is young. She is panting, writhing around, and crying out in pain. A tall nervous appearing man and a calm comforting woman accompany her. They are pushing her quickly down the hallway towards the triage room. The wheelchair zooms rapidly into the exam room, as if being driven by a race car driver. The nurse begins asking the standard medical questions; however the young woman is too distraught with pain to answer. In an instant, she begins to moan and yell out in pain as she begins to slowly slide out of the wheelchair and onto the floor. She lands on her knees. With tears streaming down her face, she looks up and exclaims, "I GOTTA PUSH!" Scurrying around, the nurses and family members try to comfort her and gently lift her off the floor. She is wrought with pain that has paralyzed her ability to voluntarily move. She is lifted off the floor by the man accompanying her, and guided onto the exam room bed. He is thin, yet muscular. He is present, yet seems disconnected—fearful and helpless.

"I gotta push!" the woman screams out! "I gotta PUUUUUSHHHH!"

"Don't push yet," the nurse shrieks desperately. "I have to check you first. I need to see how far dilated you are and make sure the baby's head is presenting first. Don't push! Just breathe through this contraction!"

The nurse grabs a pair of gloves and lubricant and prepares to do the exam.

"Hold still, focus, and breathe. Open your legs and try to relax."

As the woman continues writhing in the bed with pain, the nurse quickly performs the cervical exam.

"Head is right there," she stated as she pulled her hand back quickly. She stood up at the side of the bed, looked at the woman gently and stated,

"You're complete."

At once the young woman begins pleading aloud, "Can I push? Pleeeeeeease! I gotta push!"

"No! Not yet! Your doctor is not here. We need to call him, start an IV, and draw labs," replied the nurse.

Although important to the nurse and her fellow colleagues, who were now scrambling around the room to assist in the preparation of an imminent delivery, the only thing important to the woman in labor was pushing! She tried to contain herself, but could not! She tried to obey the instruction not to push, however, the involuntary contractions of her pelvic and rectal muscles caused her to bear down and push. It was not her intention to disobey the instruction to avoid pushing, but the urge to push was too great and she had no control over it. She continued to cry out in agony. Release and relief is all she desired. More and more the surge of contractions intensified and the pushing became more frequent! Realizing the doctor would not make it in time, the nurses prepared to deliver!

"She's crowning," the nurse shouted!

She braced herself for this miraculous yet stressful event! Calmly yet with her voice cracking, the nurse began to verbally instruct the young woman.

"Please, keep your legs open wide. This will create more room for baby. Try not to writhe around on the bed; we want a controlled delivery so that we don't risk injury to the baby. Now when you pu—"

"Aiyeeeee! Arrrgghhh!" the woman begin to scream and grunt intensely as the nurse was instructing her.

The next powerful contraction had hit. The urge was too great! The woman begins to push with full force and within seconds, a baby girl was delivered onto the field crying. It was over! It was done and the pain was gone. That young woman had become a mom! That young woman had finally entered into the journey of motherhood. That young woman was me.

Over the last few years, I've heard preachers preaching about the birthing process. Specifically, everyone seems to be focused with preaching about pushing! Leaders are commanding you who are in church to "Push out the blessings of God!" Many have also been informed that "It's time to push," and "Push now—you're in the birthing season!" Today, many are still focused on this popular public speaking topic of pushing, however they do not truly understand all that this process entails. As a board certified OB/Gyn, who has also made Christ the center of my life, answered the call to pastor, and who practices my professional passion of delivering laboring women every day, I thought it time to share both my professional expertise and God given spiritual insight into this seemingly popular preaching topic within the Kingdom of God.

While many of my colleagues within the gospel are focusing their preaching on the PUSHING stage of labor, one must first understand what has and must take place previously in one's life before the stage of pushing can ever be experienced. More specifically, one must first understand the process leading to the pushing. I have never seen a woman push a baby out who has not first been pregnant. Similarly, when it comes to birthing something spiritually, a man or woman must first identify that they are pregnant with the life-giving Word of God, before the stage of pushing can even be anticipated. Yet, I find that many believers are being commanded to push out and deliver multiple spiritual things. Things with which I'm not clear they have even been impregnated. As a result, I find many children of God frustrated and disappointed because they are not delivering what someone else has told them they should be pushing out!

So let's start here. Pregnancy. We must begin here because without it occurring first, you can never arrive at a specific time to push in the birthing process. Just like God created the human body to contain seeds that will produce new life, I believe He placed life-giving seeds in each of us when we were designed by Him. Whether a seed of an idea, or a seed that will develop into a business, ministry, company or book, we all have things that God intended for us to birth into the world. By birth I simply mean that you are manifesting something that was inside of you, outwardly for others to see and experience. What's inside of you awaiting to be birthed?

Although God designed only women with the physical ability to become pregnant; spiritual pregnancy can be experienced by both males and females. Are you ready to learn how to identify, nurture, and deliver everything you were created to do? If so, this book is for you. Whether you are a male or female, Christian or non-Christian, and regardless of whether you are medically or physically able or unable to experience "natural" childbirth, *Can I Push* will reveal your God given ability to still produce something great in this world.

Can I Push contains many real life application illustrations relating to normal pregnancy and childbirth. These illustrations were included to demonstrate the undeniable parallel between producing life obstetrically and spiritually. In this book you will discover three different sections that were created to enhance and supplement the growth you will experience throughout this amazing journey. These sections included are:

 Take A Look Inside

 Men's Perspective

 A Push Vitamin

The human body is amazing; however the intricacies of how it functions are primarily invisible to the naked eye. I have designed the ***Take A Look Inside*** segments of this book to include medical information that will reveal to you what is occurring on the inside of the body where you can't see. Although pregnancy is often thought of as a female experience, it cannot occur without the involvement of a male. As a result, the ***Men's Perspective*** has been included in *Can I Push* to reveal the genuine thoughts and feelings men may exhibit throughout the various phases of the pregnancy process they share with their loved ones. Finally, as you walk through the pages of this book, you will discover ***Push Vitamins.*** These are quotes that will be highlighted separately for you to think about more deeply. Their purpose is to provide advice or counsel that, when taken and applied regularly to your life, will supplement the growth and development you will experience throughout this process and prepare you to PUSH out greatness.

"To everything there is a season,
A time for every purpose under heaven
A time to be born. . ."

(Ecclesiastes 3:1-2)

ONE

Are You Pregnant?

Just because someone has symptoms of pregnancy doesn't mean he or she is actually pregnant—naturally or spiritually! Did you know that although men can't naturally be pregnant, they can exhibit signs and symptoms of pregnancy ranging from nausea, vomiting, and cravings; many men even experience abdominal pain that mimics contraction pain? It's true! It's called Couvade Syndrome. However, one must wonder, if people can have symptoms of pregnancy and not be pregnant, how then does one confirm whether they are indeed pregnant? The same tools needed to confirm natural pregnancy should also be utilized to determine when spiritual pregnancy is present in the lives of both men and women.

The exam room door opens. A young woman is sitting on the exam table awaiting the entrance of the doctor. She is clothed with the common white sheet draped over her legs. She appears nervous, yet excited. She is alone.

The doctor greets her with a firm handshake and warm smile.

"What brings you here today?" she inquires.

"I think I'm pregnant!" the woman replies. "My period didn't come this month, so I took a pregnancy test. It was positive."

Her eyes peer widely at the physician indicating her overwhelming desire for confirmation. The physician peers back at her with a pleasant smile. With her laptop resting on her legs, she begins to obtain a brief gynecological history from the young woman, which contains a series of questions: When was the first day of your last menstrual period? Was it normal? How long did it last? Are your periods normally regular? Have you experienced any bleeding?

The young woman begins to answer the questions. She cannot remember the specific date of her last menstrual period but definitely remembers that she did not get a period this month. She's late. For a moment she ponders the question regarding her symptoms. It is as though she is trying to organize the list in her head. She has quite a few to report and seems to be trying to determine which to announce first. She looks up suddenly and begins disclosing her list.

"In addition to my period not coming, I've also been vomiting, my breasts hurt, and I feel very tired."

"Well that sure does sound like you may be pregnant," the doctor proclaims. "Let's do an exam, and then we will order a blood test for confirmation."

Like the example above, most women will develop a suspicion that they're pregnant simply based on symptoms they begin to experience in their bodies. As a medical doctor, I know that symptoms alone are not able to confirm a pregnancy. Especially since different people may exhibit different symptoms of pregnancy. Symptoms can, however, be good indicators so I acknowledge the symptoms, but I rely on the confirmation. As a pastor, I've also learned to recognize and discern when someone may be spiritually pregnant.

Acknowledging Symptoms

One of the first signs of pregnancy for many women is a missed *menses*, or period. When a girl has her first period, this signifies that her ovaries are working and finally releasing mature eggs that can be fertilized, thus producing new life. As a result of menstruation, the lining of the uterus goes through a monthly cycle of thickening and thinning dependent upon whether or not a pregnancy occurs. A thickened lining serves as a blood rich cushion for an embryo to implant and begin to develop. When pregnancy does not occur, the thickened uterine lining will shed. This shedding manifests itself as bleeding, which a woman will experience monthly as her period. This monthly bleeding specifically indicates that new life has not occurred. It is usually something private and personal for each woman. Once the period has stopped, the process of the uterine lining becoming thickened will begin again in preparation of a possible pregnancy.

Likewise, there are many individuals in this world who appear to be living happy and well. Yet on the inside, they are quietly bleeding meaning full of hurt, disappointment, and resentment. The heaviness they carry around silently often prevents many of them from producing the fullness of life that God intended for them to live. Unbeknownst to others, they continue to silently bleed day after day, month after month. Some fall so far into despair that suicide becomes their only option. Others try to stop the bleeding by using drugs, alcohol or other means of escape.

Push Vitamin

You no longer have to live life quietly bleeding with hurts and other painful experiences. He shed His blood, so that your bleeding could stop. Release the hurts and pains of the past, and become more open to receiving what the Lord desires to deposit in you. "Give all your worry and cares to God, for He cares for you."
(1 Peter 5:7, NLT)

When Christ died on the Cross for our sins, it was *His* blood that was shed. In addition to salvation being received through the shedding of His blood, man also received grace, healing, and victory. As a result of His blood being shed, we no longer have to shed the blood of other things (animal sacrifices) to atone for our sins. Moreover, we no longer have to live life quietly bleeding with hurts and other painful experiences. He shed His blood, so that our bleeding could stop. When our bleeding stops, and we release the hurts and pains of the past, we become more open to receiving what the Lord desires to deposit in us. It is these deposits, when united with faith that cause us to become pregnant with the things of God. Therefore, similar to the natural, the cessation of bleeding (hurting, etc.) in your life can commonly be a sign of spiritual pregnancy.

Nausea and vomiting are also common symptoms of early pregnancy. These symptoms are usually related to the increase in hormones that the woman's body is responding to. Regardless of the reason, this can create a lot of unwanted liquid release (vomiting). It is a challenge to keep things down, most everything eaten seems to be released right back up out of her mouth. Some women throw up everything they eat or drink, while others may have milder symptoms.

As a physician and pastor, my medical expertise has given me the ability to recognize and discern when a believer may be spiritually pregnant. And let me tell you this, the picture is much the same as in natural pregnancy. When I see believers going through a period where they are consistently releasing everything, I suspect they're spiritually pregnant. Why? It's no different from what I see occurring in natural pregnancy. Things a woman use to consume or do before pregnancy, can no longer be tolerated. When I see believers having a difficult time ingesting and doing the things they use to do before salvation, this equates to "spiritual vomiting." These same individuals find themselves constantly having

When I see believers having a difficult time ingesting and doing the things they use to do before salvation, this equates to "spiritual vomiting."

to give up things (release them) because they are unable to tolerate or do them any longer. Their spirit becomes more sensitive to what it receives and begins to reject what is not like God. Smoking, drinking, going certain places, hanging with certain individuals, using certain kind of language, watching or listening to certain types of TV shows and music, or reading certain material become difficult to do. *Oh how the Lord will purge us!*

Finally, although other pregnancy symptoms can develop, breast tenderness is definitely another to discuss. *Ooh wee!* Talk about extreme sensitivity. If you want to see a newly pregnant woman react—touch her breast! Anything against her breast, in this stage of pregnancy, creates quite a response. Spiritually, the same symptom can and does develop.

The words breast and bosom are used interchangeably throughout the Bible. Interestingly, the word *bosom* represents and demonstrates love when used in the Word of God. Just like the breasts become extremely tender in the initial stages of pregnancy, so should our love and tenderness towards those we are in touch with. Moreover, as our sensitivity for others increases, we should also become more responsive to the needs of others. This change should be apparent in the early stages of spiritual pregnancy. By the power of the Holy Spirit, we should be able to recognize a difference in our ability to exhibit love. As a result, we should find ourselves more softhearted, affectionate, compassionate, and generous towards others.

Rely on Confirmation

Confirmation of pregnancy is essential in obstetrics. Moreover, it is important that a reliable test is performed to obtain the result. There have been times when a woman has used a home pregnancy test that yielded a positive result, only to come into my office and learn that she in fact is not pregnant. Sadly, the home pregnancy test yielded a false positive result. Likewise, vice-versa can occur, leading to women receiving a positive pregnancy result after initially obtaining a negative result from a not-so-reliable test. This is considered a false negative result.

Isn't this what happens to so many of us in our spiritual lives? We feel like God is developing something great inside of us; yet when we seek the confirmation of others, we can often be given the wrong result. This is why you cannot rely on the test of others regarding the gifts that God has placed inside of you. You must always seek a reliable source to determine or confirm if you are carrying the purpose of God for your life.

Think about it. When a woman desires to know "the truth" about whether she is pregnant or not, who does she go to for this confirmation? Answer: usually a physician or medical provider of some sort (nurse, physician assistant, midwife, etc.). In other words, she goes to someone who has studied medicine diligently and is expected to have the tools or testing necessary to provide the correct answer. Likewise, one must seek the same assuredness spiritually. Yes, there is nothing wrong with seeking confirmation concerning what you believe God is developing in you. However, please keep in mind that spiritual leaders, in the frailty of our humanness, can at times misinterpret what God is doing in the life of His people. It may not be intentional; but, like false negative test results, it occurs. This is why it is imperative that we learn to seek answers—"the Truth"—from our Lord Himself.

Push Vitamin

Don't rely solely on the ability of others to identify the gifts that God has placed inside of you. Learn to seek answers—the Truth—from the Lord Himself.

The Lord, Himself, will speak to you regarding what He has placed in you to manifest. Others should simply be confirming what your reliable source (God) has already shown you or told you. Think about it; as physicians, we are simply relaying to the patient the results that were received from the reliable test we ordered. We, ourselves, couldn't determine the answer. We had to seek the answer from something believed to be more reliable. So why should it be any different in the spiritual sense? It shouldn't.

Pregnancy tests vary in their sensitivity regarding how early they can recognize and identify the beta hCG hormone. *That's the hormone secreted in one's blood or urine when a woman is pregnant.* Sensitivity is a term that refers to—the ability of a test to detect the presence of a disease. This means, if a test has a high sensitivity, its percentage is high in its ability to positively identify a particular disease or condition. Interestingly enough, although the urine test is pretty accurate, it occasionally gives false negatives when one is testing in the very early stages of pregnancy. This is due to the fact that the pregnancy hormone level must reach a certain level in order to be detected by a home urine pregnancy test.

> ## 👀 TAKE A LOOK INSIDE:
>
> ### Why Can Test Give False Negative Results?
>
> The Beta hCG level can be detected in the urine when it has reached an average level of 20mIU. However, just because it can, doesn't mean it always will. The reason for this is due to the sensitivity of urine pregnancy tests sold in stores. Although beta hCG can be detected in the urine at a level of 20mIU, some tests are not able to do so because they have been designed by their manufacturer to recognize the hormone at a higher level. For example, some tests will be positive if at least 20mIU is present in the urine, others have been manufactured to become positive when urine levels of beta hCG are 25mIU, 40 mIU, and even 100 mIU for some test. This means that if lower levels of hormone are in the urine when the test is performed, it will give a negative result.

Certain home pregnancy tests are only able to detect the pregnancy hormone, in the urine, at a particular level. If you are pregnant and your levels have not yet reached the detectable range for that particular brand, you will get a negative result. Many individuals—like pregnancy tests—often have the same variation in sensitivity regarding their ability to detect what God has placed in others. As a result, some people aren't going to be able to recognize the giftedness that God has placed in you because it's too early. God has not caused it to manifest enough for others to identify it, because He is still developing the necessary things within you. You are still in the early stages of your development process. As a result, *people will make the mistake of thinking you are not pregnant with the things of God and give you false negatives!* If you are not careful, you will believe them and risk doing things that can compromise your pregnancy process.

Understanding the Timing of Testing

After the uniting of the egg and sperm, the developing embryo will implant underneath the lining of the uterus. This occurs usually within 5-7 days after fertilization. After implantation, the placenta begins to secrete the pregnancy hormone into the urine and blood stream. In early pregnancy (usually the first week), the levels may be very low when tested in the urine. Since urine pregnancy tests can each have a different cut-off level in which it can detect the bHCG hormone, some may give a false negative result simply because the levels in the urine have not reached a high enough level to be detected.

The serum pregnancy test, which checks for the pregnancy hormone levels in the bloodstream of a woman, is more accurate. Its accuracy is due to the blood test's ability to detect the pregnancy hormone levels when extremely low (<5mIU). With that said, this is why we (physicians) will usually use the serum (blood) pregnancy test to confirm early pregnancy in obstetrics. Like the serum pregnancy test, Jesus Christ (*"The Blood"*) is able to accurately and positively confirm what lies within each and every one —even when others themselves can't identify it. His accuracy is due to the fact that He placed the gift(s) within you when He created you.

So regarding the question, *Are you pregnant?* I believe God is the reliable source to give you your answer. The process of pregnancy is complex, yet quite divine. We leaders in the Kingdom of God should be simply serving to confirm what God has already shown you. Like most pregnant women, I believe you will know when you are spiritually pregnant. Your body will often provide you with the signs and symptoms that are often good indicators. Once pregnancy is confirmed, then you are on your way to taking a wonderful journey of spiritual development, which will ultimately lead to a need to push out a beautiful gift.

MEN'S PERSPECTIVE

Are You Pregnant?

I asked my husband, Greg, for his viewpoint regarding our first child when he realized, *we were pregnant!* I had never asked him this question before writing this book. His response gave me such insight into how men experience the pregnancy process.

Me: "What were you thinking when I started having symptoms of pregnancy but did not have test results yet?"

Greg: *"I was thinking of the future."*

Me: "What did you think or feel when you saw my pregnancy test become positive?"

I remember us both standing together in the bathroom staring at the stick, waiting.

Greg: *"Excited. Nervous. Concerned if we were prepared."*

Isn't it ironic that what men often express about natural pregnancy is similar to what many individuals feel when it comes to being spiritually pregnant? Think about how many times many of us wonder if we are ready to handle what God wants to do in us and through us as believers. Additionally, how many times have we heard someone hesitate to even come to Christ out of fear of what they believe their future will be with Him: boring, difficult to live holy, full of ridicule from others, no fun, and full of struggle. It's amazing what people think about something so wonderful, isn't it?

Likewise, even after making the decision to enter into relationship with the Lord, some of us still silently fear the beliefs we ponder regarding our future. Will people still like me? Will I lose friendships now that I've made this decision? Will I be happy? Will I fail? Will this new found faith I have reveal itself to be true or false?

For many of us, when we discovered that God was doing something new in us, we were excited yet very nervous! So don't worry if you too feel the same way—it's a normal feeling. Finally, wondering if we are prepared for what God is going to do through our lives and whether we can handle it are also common and healthy feelings. The key is that you never doubt God and His ability to complete what He promised He would do in your life. With Christ, we have everything we need to be successful—both now and in the future. Simply allow His process of growth and development to take place, knowing that He never fails. Remember, just like your partner in life, God chose you because He loves you dearly and desires to give you His best.

Two

The Release

OVULATION

So the question still remains, are you pregnant? It's not enough to think you are. You must know that you are! The reality of the matter is that there is a process that must first take place in order to lead to a confirmation of pregnancy. Have you gone through the proper process? That is the next question?

As an Obstetrician/Gynecologist, I have experienced multiple office visits with women desiring to be pregnant. Although it is a wonderful occurrence, it is not always the easiest. In fact, many women are frustrated, depressed, and even resentful towards their inability to get pregnant. Although there can be many reasons why a woman cannot get pregnant; one of the essential factors for spontaneous pregnancy to take place is healthy ovulation. The reality is that without normal ovulation, one's pregnancy capacity can be negatively impacted in a great manner.

So what is ovulation and why is it so important to the pregnancy process? The ovulation process is simply the release of a mature egg, *known as the ovum*, from a woman's ovary. This egg is what is needed to unite with a male sperm in order to produce a desired pregnancy. Without the release of this egg, a normal pregnancy can never take place.

So let's stop for a moment! The word I want to focus on right now is *release*! When the egg is released from the ovary, it breaks through and out of the ovary itself. Pregnancy cannot take place without a release—natural or spiritual! Preachers are constantly teaching the Body of Christ that we must be pregnant with the things of God! Although I agree, my medical knowledge allows me to make the spiritual parallel, that pregnancy with the things of God cannot take place until there has been a spiritual release. So, what do I mean by spiritual release? Likely, something very different than what you may think.

Throughout the Kingdom of God, we have constantly been referring to the need of the believer to have a breakthrough! Ironically, the word breakthrough does not appear anywhere in the Bible (NKJV). Only the phrase "break through"—*two words*—appears in the Bible in five separate verses. Interestingly enough, in all five verses, this phrase is simply referring to one's ability to "get pass" something (Exodus 19:21, 24; 2 Kings 3:26; Matthew 6:19, 20, NKJV). Despite this truth, we still hear the term "breakthrough" used to mean "one receiving a victory moment" in the midst of a struggle. At times, I've heard preachers seemingly using the word "breakthrough" synonymously with the word "deliverance," as if to say getting a "breakthrough" equates with being or receiving one's deliverance in a particular area. This seems to be an incomplete use of the word.

Now, when I refer to the physiological process of pregnancy, I want to remind you that what is breaking through and being released from the ovary is a mature egg. Notice I said, mature. This egg must be fertilized by a male sperm, if pregnancy is going to take place during a particular menstrual cycle and create new life. The word sperm is derived from the Greek word "*sperma* which literally means *seed, from speiren* meaning to sow *(Merriam-Webster online dictionary)*." This is why sperm is often referred to as the seed of a man. Fertilization of the mature egg by the male seed is essential to reproducing new life. Specifically, a new life in which one's purpose will be revealed and greatness will be manifested.

So as a result of what must take place in the natural, I believe the same process must take place in the spiritual. With that said, I believe that the spiritual parallel is this: the mature egg that is released from a woman's ovary, is like mature faith that is released from one's spirit. When this mature faith breaks through one's Spirit, it is now free to be fertilized by the Seed, Jesus Christ (Galatians 3:16, NKJV).

Luke 18:8 asks, "When the Son of Man comes back, will he find faith on the earth?" I ask myself, "Why would He be looking for faith as oppose to something else?" My answer is, that I believe faith is the substance whereby all things are created and produced. Just like a mature egg must be released to create a baby, mature faith must exist to create newness (or birth anything new) in our lives. Therefore, I have concluded that spiritual pregnancy cannot occur without faith. Simply put: no egg—no baby. Likewise, no faith—no (spiritual) baby! Rarely, if ever, can I think of a time in the Bible when Christ performed a miracle in the presence of individuals who did not possess faith.

This faith however, must be mature, just like the egg released from a woman's ovary must be mature. A mature egg, medically speaking, is one that has grown to a certain size and produced certain characteristics. Similarly enough, the Bible tells us that every man has been given "the measure of faith." Notice that the verse states "the" versus "a" measure of faith. This implies, that the portion of faith given to one by God is identical to the measure of faith that God gives to another. In other words, everyone is given the same exact amount—the measure—of faith. The truth of the matter lies in what one does with this measure of faith. Faith needs to grow and mature throughout our walk with Christ. Once we begin to release mature faith, we will then be able to produce the fullness of God into every situation of our lives, when it's unified with the Seed of Christ.

Push Vitamin

When you release mature faith that unites with the Seed of Christ, you will produce the fullness of God into every situation of your life.

Matthew 17:19-20 demonstrates that we need a mature faith. When the disciples, in the face of their failure to cast out the demon, asked Jesus "Why weren't we able to cast the demon out of the boy?" Jesus responded, "Your faith was too little." Wow! Notice that it was not that faith was absent. It was that faith was too little—or not big enough.

If God were to examine your faith, would He say "it was too little or not enough?"

In other words, not mature. Faith is essential for the children of God because without it, one cannot have relationship with God. Faith is the foundation of Christianity, and it is "by faith" that salvation is received. We are justified by and through faith and without faith it is impossible to please God.

So how does faith become mature in order that when it's released it will set out to accomplish what it was meant to do: create new life? Ironically, the maturing of faith is no different than the maturing of the ovum (egg released from the ovary). In the natural, there are multiple actions working together in what I believe to be a divine process that causes an egg to mature. These actions involve various stimulating hormones working together, on and within the ovary to create a mature egg that will become dominant and be released. James 2:22 states, "Do you see that faith was working together with his works, and by works faith was made perfect?" The Greek word used in this scripture for the word *perfect* is *teleieoo*, meaning "complete" or "mature." The spiritual parallel for me is that faith must also be accompanied by actions to mature. This is essential to our spiritual pregnancy because if mature faith cannot be released, pregnancy is not possible. Why is pregnancy not possible? Well remember, it takes a fertilized egg to develop into a pregnancy. If no egg is released, you've got it, it's impossible for normal pregnancy to occur because there is nothing to be fertilized by the sperm.

Up to this point, I've been emphasizing the fact that a "mature" egg must be released in order for natural pregnancy to occur. But I must say, that I wondered, *what would happen if an immature egg was released?* It was through my research and discussion with two of my Reproductive Endocrinology colleagues that I discovered a profound reality. Through the knowledge of this phenomenal reality, an amazing spiritual revelation was illuminated to me. You see, I learned that human ovaries do not normally release immature eggs. In fact, when the menstrual cycle is working fully and without compromise, only mature eggs are released. This is simply the way God designed the female body to function. In the normal setting, if a mature egg is not available to be released ovulation does not occur. This means nothing is released that month, and there is no possibility of something being produced that cycle.

Nothing is released! Some of you may be thinking—*but why?* My answer: *because it can't!* You see, the release of the mature egg from the ovary is not dependent on the function of the ovary alone. Actually, it is the brain that is primarily responsible for the release of the mature egg. Allow me to reveal this truth further.

First you must understand that at birth, a baby girl's ovaries already contain immature eggs. They lie dormant within a hollow cell called a follicle until she starts having menstrual cycles. At the initiation of the menstrual cycle, a small number of follicles are recruited to undergo the process of maturation. The ovary recruits them based on their sensitivity to a hormone called Follicle Stimulating Hormone (FSH). Once these follicles are triggered to start maturing, they begin to release a hormone called estrogen. Estrogen triggers an area of the brain, and when the brain receives this signal from the follicle it releases specific hormones that will cause maturation of the immature egg. Although multiple follicles were recruited, only one will be selected to be the dominant follicle. Dominant meaning that it will be the follicle to produce and release the mature egg. As the brain continues to stimulate the ovary to mature the egg that has been selected to be released (ovulated), the maturing egg continues to produce more and more estrogen. In response, the brain releases a huge surge of a hormone that directly generates the release of the mature egg from the follicle and ovary. The initially recruited immature eggs that did not survive the process will fizzle away.

> 👀 **TAKE A LOOK INSIDE:**
>
> ### How Does An Egg Mature?
>
> When a baby girl is born her ovaries contain hundreds of thousand follicles (immature eggs) just waiting for the time to come when they will be matured and released. Ovulation is a part of the menstrual cycle in which the ovary releases a mature egg. The process involved in ovulation is complex and involves not only the ovaries but also the brain. During the first few days of a woman's menstrual cycle, the brain releases hormones that will stimulate the follicles to begin to mature the egg that lies within it. This hormone is called FSH (Follicle Stimulating Hormone). As the follicles are stimulated by this hormone, they begin to release estrogen as they begin to grow. Finally, one follicle is chosen to be the dominant follicle. This means it's been selected to release the mature egg for that menstrual cycle. This chosen follicle begins to release a large amount of estrogen which not only causes the egg to mature quickly, but stimulates the brain to release a surge of a hormone called the Luteinizing Hormone (LH). It is this surge of LH which is directly responsible for the release of the mature egg from the ovary. Without this LH surge, the mature egg will not be released.

My God! This corresponds directly to the scripture "many are called but few are chosen" (Matthew 20:16, NKJV). Like the follicles that are initially recruited, God calls many of us to come, grow, and mature in Him. The problem is that many of us fail to develop the necessary faith to believe in what God promises. As a result, many of us choose not to come to Him at all, or if we do come—we don't stay. We fizzle away due to our lack of faith.

Like the ovary, I believe that God purposed for believers to consistently release mature faith. The problem however, is that we often allow our mindsets to affect the maturing of our faith instead of allowing our faith to affect our mindset! Remember, when immature eggs are triggered to become mature, they begin releasing a small amount of hormone that causes the brain to release the substance necessary for the egg to fully mature and be released. Our faith responds no differently. The Word of God says that if you just have a small amount of faith, you can move mountains (Matthew 17:20, NKJV). The scripture further states, "nothing will be impossible for you." Why? Because it takes only a small amount of faith to activate the transformation of your mind. In challenging times, if you could just allow your spirit to hold onto the small amount of faith that you do have, I promise that faith will generate a mindset change that will produce a greater or mature faith.

Although faith is necessary to our growth, mindset is critical to our maturation. Only a small amount of faith is needed to produce the atmosphere necessary for our minds to be transformed so that we can mature in Christ. When your mindset changes, you will begin to have the mind of Christ. When you have the mind of Christ, you move to a place of knowing God. It is the knowing and believing from the mind that automatically produces your ability to release mature faith. I liken it to the Follicle Stimulating Hormone (FSH) that is released from the brain to signal the ovary to mature the egg. I believe the Holy Spirit's power stimulates and transforms our minds to release a Faith Stimulating Hormone (spiritual FSH) to signal our spirits to produce and generate mature faith. *Mindset is a powerful thing.*

Now, in the rare circumstances that an immature egg happens to be released, it is due to an irregularity in the body that has caused a hormonal imbalance. In the event that an immature egg is released and fertilized, it is unable to produce viable life.

Now then, here goes the revelation behind this. The Bible says, "first natural and then spiritual." Therefore, if God designed the human body (of a woman) to only release mature eggs to be fruitful, multiply and replenish, then spiritually speaking we should do the same. I am amazed that the saints of God continue to release immature faith, yet still have a full expectation to produce and ultimately birth the things of God. Ironically, what they have not realized is that nothing viable will come forth. The problem is not in the Word of God which is complete and perfect, the problem is the individual who lacks faith.

Likewise, faith without the necessary works will not mature, and as scripture so clearly outlines, this faith is dead (James 2:26, NKJV). As we say in the field of obstetrics, it is *non-viable*. At times, the inability for a woman to get pregnant is due to the fact that her ovaries are not ovulating properly. In my field, we call that "anovulation." Simply put, it means a mature egg is not being released monthly. The symptom manifested is often a woman complaining that she does not have monthly menstruation, or she may report that it comes every other month, every few months or not at all.

Well, like the female egg was designed to be release monthly, I believe mature faith must also be "released" regularly for the believer to even have the ability to be pregnant with the things of God on a regular basis. Likewise, I believe this is the reason why many people within the kingdom of God are frustrated with their lack of ability to birth the things of God. When the ovum is not released regularly, one is at risk for infertility. So it is with the spiritual body. If faith is not released in the believer consistently, then the believer likewise is at risk of spiritual infertility, which can lead to a life long struggle of barrenness. As a result, engaging in sexual activity will not matter, because the issue is not connectedness (or intimacy) but it's the lack of release.

Many believers are having encounters with God, but nothing is produced or manifested outwardly. Why? Maybe it's because, the believer is having intercourse (connectedness) with God without the faith that He can and will produce something good within him or her. Oh yes! I've seen it many times! As a pastor, I have met individuals who truly love God, who truly want to live holy, who truly desire to obey God, and who desire the purpose of God for their lives. These individuals are truly anointed by God. They truly serve God wholeheartedly and are authentic disciples of God, yet they struggle to birth forth the things of God in the earth. Why? Because they, like the disciples, have too little faith or they release no faith. "They have the form of Godliness, but deny the power thereof" (2 Tim 3:5, NKJV). They struggle to believe that there is greatness and purpose that God has placed in them to be birthed outwardly for others to receive. As a result, doubt and low self esteem prevent the release of faith from their spirit. This results in the inability to reproduce what God placed inside.

So how do we increase our faith so that it can be released regularly? Romans 10:17 says, "Faith comes by hearing and hearing by the Word of God." How do we "hear" the Word of God? Do we go purchase an audio Bible? Do we read the Bible out loud? Do we open the Bible, stare at it and wait for it to speak? *Ok, I confess I have always wanted to have the testimony of hearing an audible voice come from my Bible!* Whereas these are great ways to hear the scriptures, the Bible tells

Push Vitamin

You must regularly "hear" the Word of God. By hearing the Word of God, your faith will be increased.

us that we hear the 'Word of God' by hearing and listening to Jesus. How do we know this for sure? Let's take a closer look at Romans 10:17.

Notice in Romans 10:17, "Word" begins with a capital letter. Based on the rules of grammar, the only reason to capitalize the first letter of a word is to depict the name or title of a person, place, or proper/branded thing. This means this verse is trying to reveal a specific identity, otherwise, if the word "Word" refers to the normal words we use to communicate in everyday language, it would not need to be capitalized and the entire word would, thus, be written in all lower case letters. Still with me? Great! We know that the "Word of God" is not a place, and it seems that this passage of scripture reveals the <u>*personification*</u> of the Word of God. As a result, we can rule out that the "Word of God" is a thing. Don't believe me? Well, where else is a capital 'W' used in the phrase "Word of God?" Let's look at John 1:1. It states, "In the beginning was the Word, and the Word was with God, and the Word was God. He was in the beginning with God (NKJV)." Now, this verse clearly reveals that "the Word" is a person, not a thing. It says "the Word" was with God, "the Word" was God, and then ends defining "the Word" as a "He" in the final sentence which reads, "He was in the beginning with God."

Whew! Grammar lesson is now over and we know that "the Word" is a person. But *who* is this person that is named "the Word?" *Drum roll please!* The "Word of God" is Jesus Christ Himself! How do we know for sure? The answer lies in the verse John 1:14. It begins with "And the Word became flesh and dwelt among us, and we beheld His glory, the glory as of the only begotten of the Father..." Boom! There it is! We know that Jesus Christ was the Word made flesh and that our Father God sent Him to this earth in physical form to dwell among us. We also know that Jesus Christ was with God in the beginning and is His only "begotten Son," as He is referred to throughout multiple scriptures in the Bible.

So why did I take time to go through all of this? What does this have to do with faith and becoming pregnant with the things of God? Remember, we discussed that a mature faith must be released regularly from one's Spirit if the potential for spiritual pregnancy is to occur. Like women who seek help regarding their inability to ovulate and release mature eggs, so must we seek spiritual assistance or guidance from a pastor or church leader when we too find ourselves with difficulty in releasing mature faith. In obstetrics and gynecology, there are multiple conditions that can affect a woman's ability to develop mature eggs. The key however is that with the help of treatment and other assistance, many will not only generate mature eggs, but also obtain pregnancy. Likewise the same is true spiritually. With assistance, many will not only generate mature faith, but can also go on to obtain spiritual pregnancy.

When mature faith is lacking, so is the potential for us to be pregnant with the things of God. If faith is to be increased, we learned earlier that this occurs from one "hearing by the Word of God," or more specifically, hearing Christ. In order to hear someone, you must be within a certain proximity to them, usually close! This would mean, that in order for one's faith to be matured, one must be close to Christ, meaning one must be in relationship with Christ and having intimacy with Him. I believe that many in the Kingdom of God are unable to become pregnant with the things of God because they are not fully recognizing that the "Word of God" is not a *what*, but a *who*. As a result, they are hearing "words" but not "the Word" of God. Immature faith becomes matured through the help and treatment of the Word of God. This Word of God can be administered through the Sunday morning or other sermons, corporate or personal bible study, and fellowship with others. Many times we fail to make the Word (Christ) alive in our lives. We are connected to the words spoken or read by men, but are not connected or in relationship with the Word Himself. As a result, our faith cannot be increased, because Christ is not being heard. We are focusing on the actual text itself, and not *who* it actually is.

MEN'S PERSPECTIVE

Ovulation

In thinking about ovulation, I wondered what a man really thinks about this solely female process. After all, most men have grown up with or have been around a woman and are therefore familiar with its symptoms. Through a phone texting conversation, my husband, Greg, and I discussed this topic.

Me: *You had three women living in the house with you. What comes to mind when you hear the word, ovulation?*

Greg: *Trouble. Watch out. Stay clear. Tread lightly. Provide an extra dose of patience and avoid bombshells.*

Me: *What does avoid bombshells mean?*

Greg: *It means, if I hear a loaded question or situation, try to avoid!*

I don't think I was prepared for his response. I guess it's what most men feel regarding ovulating women, they're often not prepared for our response. It's true many women have very emotional journeys during the process leading up to the release of a mature egg. Until the time for release to occur, the egg is still considered immature. This time of immaturity is commonly the time when women will exhibit the famous Pre Menstrual Syndrome (PMS) symptoms. You know what I mean—irritability, moodiness, and hypersensitivity. Some of us, at this time tend to also complain more. I must admit, during this time, our emotions can be very labile. As a result, I can understand why men may feel the desire to *stay clear*!

Like the ovum, that is maturing during a women's menstrual

cycle, so our faith, as believers, must also mature in order to produce Christ like life. During our journey from immaturity to maturity, we all can exemplify behavior that makes others uneasy and at times uncomfortable. Wavering faith always produces doubt. Doubt can make people do and say things that trouble people—including God. Furthermore, when you struggle with doubt, you will often ask many loaded questions. Take for example the woman who asks her husband, after putting on that special outfit, "Do I look fat in this?" Or that husband who asks his wife, "Why did you marry me?" Often times, these loaded questions are nothing more than vehicles to arguments and complaints. This results in people feeling the need to *tread lightly* in conversation with us, or to avoid it altogether.

When a young girl experiences her first period, it is normal for the subsequent periods to come irregularly instead of every month. This is due to the communication between the brain and the ovary still needing to mature. In fact, as gynecologists we often document the cause in these cases as, Immature Hypothalamic Pituitary Ovarian Axis. It results in the lack of a mature egg being released because the immature communication between the brain and the ovary prevents ovulation—a release. I usually counsel the child's parents that intervention is not necessary at this time. Only patience and time to develop are usually required at this point.

Spiritually, I see the same thing occurring in the men and women of God. While our faith is maturing it can go through a phase of wavering. You know, here today, gone tomorrow. Sometimes we will release mature faith, sometimes we won't. Similar to young girls, this irregularity is common and to be expected during the early life of a believer, because the communication between the body, soul, and spirit is still immature. Developing mature faith can also be a process. However, as a young girl becomes older, the expectation is that she will begin to ovulate regularly because the communication between her brain and ovary has matured. So it should be with the children of God. As we grow in the Lord, the release of mature faith should also become more regular and apparent. As a result, there should be less displays of doubt, anxiety, anger, and any other responses that often cause others to avoid us and God. Remember, without faith it is impossible to please God. As we begin to communicate more with God through His word and by the Word, we should begin to demonstrate an attitude that draws others towards us, and ultimately Christ.

Three

The Encounter

INTERCOURSE

Sex! Sex! Sex! Our culture has revolutionized sex in such a way that most are no longer aware of its original purpose. Sex is performed amongst the old and amongst the young. Sex is performed in and out of marriage. Sex is performed with and without love. Sex is performed with and without commitment. Sex is performed in private and in public. Sex seemingly has no boundaries and has dominated our society in such a way that is indescribable. Sex is everywhere! It has infiltrated every aspect of our culture, including our churches.

People do not get pregnant by themselves. Not in the normal sense. Pregnancy requires a relationship of some sort, whether good or bad. All relationships develop out of some type of encounter, whether pleasant or negative. This could be an encounter on a job, or in the mall, or could be an encounter arranged by other people desiring to play matchmaker. The word "encounter" is defined as "a meeting or an experience" (Merriam-Webster online dictionary). It's how two individuals initially meet. The word itself, although it can encompass sex, is not limited to this type of encounter by any means. There are business encounters, medical encounters, professional encounters, scientific encounters, etc. Simply put, encounters serve as the manner in which people come into contact with each other. However this occurs, one cannot get around the fact that, the inception of a relationship requires a meeting of some type between people.

Now as it pertains to pregnancy, a sexual encounter must first take place. This means that at some point the initial encounter of two individuals becomes more intimate. And it is through this sexual encounter that intercourse takes place. This relationship can advance into a sexual encounter slowly or immediately, but that is determined by the individuals themselves.

Are you sexually active? How many sexual partners have you had in the last 6 months? In the last year? As an OB/Gyn, I have the responsibility of asking these, and other necessary questions to each patient. Yes! I know these are considered private and confidential questions that can make some individuals uncomfortable. Nevertheless, I must ask in order to assess one's risks for specific infections that can not only cause illness, but can inhibit one's ability to get pregnant if left undetected and untreated.

Throughout my years of practicing medicine, it is evident that more individuals are having sex than those that are not. Surprisingly enough, sexual intercourse is occurring amongst individuals of all ages, even among our pre-teenagers. My youngest pregnant patient was 12 years old. *She was eleven when she got pregnant, twelve when she delivered.* My oldest woman with a sexually transmitted disease was 80 years old. It was heartbreaking to have to tell her she had developed the Herpes virus from her last sexual encounter. It was even more devastating to see her sobbing over the fact that trust had been broken between her and someone she thought she "knew."

Knew. When the Bible is referring to sexual intercourse between two individuals, the word "knew" is used to represent this experience. Examples of this are seen in Genesis 4:1, "Now Adam knew Eve his wife, and she conceived…" and Genesis 4:17, "And Cain knew his wife, and she conceived, and bore Enoch." The word "knew" is used this way to depict a very "intimate relationship that includes ardor and passion but also mutuality and oneness. This was an act of procreation" (*NKJV Study Bible Commentary notes, pg. 10*).

Spontaneous pregnancy, meaning unassisted, cannot occur without an unprotected sexual encounter between a male and female. It's impossible. When God told Adam and Eve to "be fruitful, multiply, replenish" (Gen. 1:26), He was speaking to their mandate to reproduce. Human reproduction requires a sexual encounter to take place. This is a necessary element in the process to becoming pregnant, because without it, there can be no uniting of the sperm and ovary to produce a new creature (new life). Remember, once the mature egg is released from the ovary, it is now awaiting fertilization by the seed of a male partner – sperm. Now there are times in the medical field, where certain types of conditions can inhibit a male or female's ability to reproduce naturally during a sexual encounter. In some of these instances, medical assistance is implemented to aid in the development of new life. Nevertheless, the fact remains, that an encounter—be it sexual or medical—is required for pregnancy to be possible. It is only through these encounters that the sperm and egg have an opportunity to meet. Therefore, if a sexual encounter is needed for the possibility of pregnancy to occur naturally, then spiritually speaking, an encounter of some sort must take place for you to become pregnant with the things of God.

So my next question to you is, "Are you in a relationship with someone in whom you are at risk of becoming pregnant?" "How many partners have you had sex with in the last year? Or last month?" *What?* That question is just as important spiritually as it is naturally. Don't get freaked out by the fact that I'm using the word "sex" or "sexual encounter" when referring to spiritual things. Didn't God create sex? In case you forgot, He did! Additionally, please keep in mind that the basic definition of sexual intercourse is the physical contact between two individuals during which their reproductive organs connect. When carried out in the way God designed it, a sexual encounter that leads to a completed act of sexual intercourse should lead to pregnancy. So, back to my question. How many lifetime partners have you had sexual encounters with? Would you say one? Two? Or maybe more? Are you offended by my question? Great! That means we are tapping into a sensitive area that may need to be explored; especially if you desire to birth forth and push out the things of God. Again, who are you with? I can't say it enough.

Who you become sexually involved with, is often who you become connected to spiritually and emotionally. Moreover, intercourse with this person also determines the image and characteristics of the new person who will be created and manifested. What is manifested derives from what's represented in the DNA of those connected through intercourse. In other words: whatever is birthed will reflect and manifest the DNA of its parents. *Looks. Personality. Behavior. They're all determined by DNA.*

Who you become sexually involved with, is who you become connected to spiritually and emotionally.

I must challenge you to look at *who* your encounters are with. This is important because it affects many facets of the pregnancy process. As a physician, it can help me to determine if the pregnancy is at risk for complications. These complications can involve infections, abnormal development of the fetus, and what will ultimately be manifested at time of delivery. These encounters, especially if negative, can also cause psychological trauma that can jeopardize the continuance of a

Push Vitamin

I challenge you to take a look at who your encounters are with. Whether sexual or platonic; spiritual or professional; a basic friendship or social media "friend," examine the relationships you have.

pregnancy.

Who my patients are partnered with can impact the pregnancy process in so many ways. I ask them if they are partnered with a supportive and loving individual or with someone who is abusive or absent. I want to know if they are partnered with someone who is mature and can handle the responsibilities of a new baby. Are they in a healthy relationship or a relationship where they are being influenced negatively (doing drugs, engaged in criminal activity)? Finally, it is important, to me, to know that my patient is partnered with someone who can provide for her and the gift that will be birthed in the future.

So what is the spiritual parallel to all this "encounter" talk? Well, if you desire to be pregnant with the things of God, then I believe you must first have a relationship with God. Just like the natural—so it is in the spiritual. *People cannot get pregnant by themselves.* Likewise, an encounter with God is required for you to become pregnant with the things of God. *Contrary to what many believe, an encounter with God does not have to take place in a church.* It can take place anywhere and at any time. God will often meet you where you are. He is constantly pursuing us with His love. When we accept His love and Son (Jesus Christ) through faith, a relationship is established and new life begins. As the relationship with God grows, there should be a hunger and thirst for Him that causes you to desire to know Him at a deeper level. As this intimacy grows, it should cause a stirring inside of you that causes you to develop the passionate desire for Him to be in you, and you to be in Him completely. This is what I define as spiritual intercourse.

Oh no! There I go again—mixing spiritual and sexual stuff! Stay with me! Remember we are talking about pushing out the things of God; however, as we mentioned earlier, you cannot push out anything unless you are pregnant! As a result, we are walking through the process of pregnancy so that we can truly understand its process and determine if you are in fact pregnant with the things of God. I know you have the seeds to produce, but who are you uniting with to ultimately manifest the greatness in you? Is it God? Is it others? That's important. Don't get uncomfortable with the terms, just continue to follow the parallelism of the process spiritually. If you miss the process whereby natural pregnancy occurs, you will miss the process of how spiritual pregnancy occurs—which is the same.

Remember God invented intercourse and I believe it was always meant to be spiritual, as well as natural. The problem is that our society has chosen to disconnect the act of intercourse from God and focus on the natural aspect of it. Moreover society, from the influence of the devil, has taken this very spiritual act and perverted it in ways that have prevented people (including Christians) from fully understanding its spiritual importance. Intercourse is all about becoming one. Many are not aware that intercourse creates a union between the spirits of two individuals. This is why sex outside of marriage is so dangerous! This danger lies in the ability for soul ties to be created that, for many, keep them in emotional and spiritual bondage. As a result, we find many people with "soul ties" to individuals that they cannot free themselves of despite their desire to do so. Why? Because the spiritual connectedness that has been formed is too great to overcome, even when the connection has a negative impact on one's life.

Intercourse is more than just the physical contact between two bodies coming together. I'm sure you've heard the saying, "when you sleep with someone, you also sleep with everyone else they've slept with." *Sleep meaning to have sex.* If you weren't aware, this is a paraphrase from one of our former U.S. Surgeon Generals, Dr. C. Everett Koop. Matter of fact his full quote is, "When you have sex with someone, you are having sex with everyone they have had sex with for the last ten years, and everyone they and their partners have had sex with for the last ten years." Wow! Talk about indirect exposure to conditions that can negatively affect you. If this can occur medically, surely it can happen spiritually. Like the former U.S. Surgeon General who has already warned our society medically; God Himself has also warned us spiritually of this risk. This is why He instructs us to avoid fornication and adultery. Same risks naturally, pertain to us spiritually.

Now, you may have noticed me using the word "completed" at various times when referring to intercourse. Intercourse, when completed, is about penetration and often the transference of one's seed of life to another individual (sperm deposit). Moreover, completed intercourse involves the stimulation and awakening of multiple organs that ultimately creates a sexual response. Although this sexual encounter may have been initiated voluntarily, it climaxes involuntarily.

Over the years, I have led multiple workshops and lectures for major hospital systems and marriage conferences regarding human sexual response. This topic was first studied, in the 1950's, by two cutting edge researchers named Dr. William Masters and Dr. Virginia Johnson. These two individuals studied the physiological responses that occurred in the human body by observing couples while they engaged in sexual activities. Throughout my medical and spiritual career I have used my presentation, "Spice Up Your Sex Life," to help individuals learn how their bodies respond sexually. Although the human sexual response during intercourse is complex; I want to take a moment to highlight the basic overview of it.

Masters and Johnson, through their scientific research, discovered four stages of sexual response: Excitement, Plateau, Orgasm, and Resolution. Through this data, we have learned that during intercourse heart rate, breathing, blood pressure, and vaginal lubrication increases. Additionally, there is a repositioning of the uterus from a tilted forward to an upright and erect position. Other physiological changes that occur include engorgement of the genitalia (the clitoris and lips of the vagina) that takes place as more blood flow travels to the area. Finally, rhythmic pelvic contractions involving the uterus and the vagina develop as the climax of the sexual response is reached. These contractions also cause the pelvis and the hips to rock back and forth. Additionally, these rhythmic contractions cause the cervix (the opening to the womb) to begin to dip downward into the fluid (the ejaculate) that has been released inside of the vaginal canal. All of these things, although physiological, are involuntary.

Spiritually speaking, I believe that worship is the equivalent to sexual intercourse. Although my reasons for this belief are multiple, primarily it is because I cannot deny the medical parallel to this spiritual experience. Remember, we are walking through the process of how one becomes pregnant in the natural, and paralleling it to the spiritual. With that said, it is important to understand that intercourse is a very important element of both the natural and spiritual process of conceiving. Likewise, God designed and purposed for this experience to be intimate. Intercourse is not limited to physical sexual contact, but can also mean an "exchange of thoughts or feelings: communion" (i.word.com dictionary). Worship is a very personal and intimate expression of love and adoration towards God. However, just like sexual intercourse, worship generates pleasure that is mutually experienced by those involved in its action. God gets great pleasure from our praise and worship, and we indeed experience pleasure when worshiping. Though many may initially engage in the act of intercourse voluntarily, at some point the stimulation of the body by this very act generates an involuntary response that affects one's entire body.

Likewise, worship does the same thing. We enter into it voluntarily (with voluntary movement). We begin praising and celebrating our Lord physically. Many of us start off on our knees, or bowed (tilted forward) before the Lord. Others may commence their worship with the clapping or the raising of their hands to the Lord. Similar to intercourse, as we continue deeper into this worship experience, our spirit begins to often generate an involuntary response, which affects our entire body. These involuntary responses may involve crying, groaning, yelling, rhythmic rocking or even shaking. The book of Psalms demonstrates many of these responses to praising and worshiping our God. Psalms 33:1 instructs the people of God to "rejoice in the Lord" (NKJV). The Hebrew word for "rejoice" in this scripture literally means, "to give a ringing cry (in joy, exhortation, distress)" (Strong's Concordance, H7442). This type of cry represents an impulsive singing or shouting that emits spontaneously from the believer during worship. It's unplanned and unexpected. *Similar to what individuals may experience at a certain point during sex.* It often occurs when we begin to feel full (or engorged) with His spirit. Praising and worshiping God with our hands (extending and lifting them up) is known as Yadah *(yaw-daw)* and Towdah *(tow-daw)* (Strong's Concordance H3034, H8426).

    Finally, for some during worship, there is a repositioning of their posture, often moving from the tilted over position of bowing to one of uprightness or erectness while standing tall with both hands stretched upward toward heaven in surrender. In Psalm 95:6, believers are invited to bow down and kneel before the Lord (NKJV). The Hebrew words for this type of worship are *Kara* (to bow down) and *Barak* (to kneel). Others may find themselves laying prostrate before the Lord.

God is attracted to our worship (Psalm 22:3), and as a result, it causes Him to draw closer. When we fully engage in worship, it causes our heart and spirit to open more and more to receive the things that the Lord desires to deposit into us. Our decision to enter into relationship with Him allows God to "set His seal of ownership on us, and put his Spirit in our hearts as a deposit, guaranteeing what is to come" (2 Corinthians 1:22, NIV).

Worship gives God permission to deposit more of Himself and His Spirit into us.

Push Vitamin

Worship gives God permission to deposit more of Himself and His Spirit into us.

You must get comfortable with worship!

Therefore, as we worship the Lord, He reveals more of Himself to us, allowing us to "know" Him even more. Intercourse between man and woman always involves "revealing" more of one's self to each other, be it emotional vulnerabilities or physical exposure. This is a loving experience. An experience intended to be authentic and based on true commitment. An authentic loving and intimate relationship with God will always lead to a spiritual deposit that ultimately leads to individuals becoming pregnant with the things of God. *God is all about reproducing.*

In reality, not all intercourse contains love and intimacy. For some it has become routine, burdensome, and even a time of hypocrisy. Yes, hypocrisy. I'm sure we all know individuals who have said they faked enjoying sex with a partner or spouse. Even worse, some have faked having the ultimate orgasm. Maybe you yourself have done it. Well, believers do the same thing. They go through the motions in church of having an encounter with God that may not be as authentic as one may display. Many yell, jump, quiver, and cry. Yet it is nothing more than an emotional facade to cover an empty relationship. Empty, meaning no intimacy, no healthy communication, and no connection—just two people, often living in the same home, going through the motions of marriage, but absolutely no connection physically, emotionally, or spiritually.

As a marriage ministry founder and coach for more than 13 years, I've been surprised to learn that individuals could and would live together with absolutely no connection or engagement between each other. On the outside, they would put on their happy face and go through the motions saying, "everything is great." However, behind the closed doors of their homes and hearts the picture was very different. There is no love, intimacy, or intercourse taking place.

Many do the same thing in their relationship with God. They put on an *appearance of Godliness*. They look and act like they are in faithful, loving, and intimate relationships with God; however, the reality is that their relationship with God has gone cold. There is no communication (prayer). There is no intimacy and connectedness (relationship). Bluntly stated, there is no worship (intercourse) with God, which is why they cannot get pregnant with the things of God.

So what are some other reasons that an encounter with God

does not lead to one's ability to conceive and birth forth the things of God? Let's look at Genesis 4:1 and 4:17 again. If you look carefully, you will see that in both passages the result of intercourse was that the woman conceived. She became pregnant. This same trend occurs many times throughout the Bible, making it evident that God's original purpose for intercourse was to result in conception and pregnancy.

Historically, man has always found a way to reject the purpose of God in his life. The area of pregnancy has been no different. There is not a day that goes by in my profession, that I am not having a consultation with a patient regarding her desire to start contraception. That is, birth control. It has become the primary way that individuals around the world prevent pregnancy while having their desired sexual encounters.

Another reason for its use is to decrease the risk of sexually transmitted diseases. In my field, using contraception is often called "using protection." Medically speaking, it is a means to inhibit the natural process that results in pregnancy. More specifically, a part of the process is blocked, whether it's suppressing the normal function of the ovaries to prevent ovulation (the release), or blocking the ability of sperm to unite with the ovary (fertilization). Nevertheless, the result is still the same: unfruitfulness. Sadly to say, many times contraception is needed because we as a society have lost our ability to control our sexual appetite and utilize intercourse in the way that God purposed it.

Like myself, I am sure that many of you have used contraception at some point in your lifetime. The question is have you brought that "contraception" mindset into your spiritual life? Remember, contraception is a safeguard that prevents pregnancy. Most people asking me for birth control are asking because:

- They are afraid to get pregnant at that time in their life
- They do not want the responsibility of taking care of a child right then.
- They are too busy with work or other personal goals.
- They just want to enjoy the pleasure of sex and nothing more.
- They want to be "safe" from developing infections arising from unfaithfulness within the relationship.

As a physician, it is not my place to judge one's reason for using birth control. Truthfully, I am an advocate for contraception. In fact, I often encourage it in women who I know are not ready to handle pregnancy and the upbringing of a child. These women are usually teenagers; people with high-risk medical illnesses; those that are demonstrating high levels of immaturity and risky behavior (drug addictions, prostitution, and constant imprisonment); people with the inability to care for the children they currently have; and women in abusive relationships.

Naturally speaking, I believe everyone must make their own decisions concerning birth control. Spiritually speaking, I don't believe we need these same safeguards as it pertains to our relationship and intimacy with Christ. In actuality, I believe that the "contraception mindset" that has infiltrated our churches, is responsible for the unfruitfulness of many children of God, because they are having "protected" spiritual intercourse. Think about it, many believers are guarded within their relationship with Christ. As a result, they struggle with trust and the belief that God will be faithful to them. Although they truly love God, their fear inhibits their very ability to worship freely and completely in the Lord. As a result, their desire to "protect" themselves, personal goals, dreams, and their safety often inhibits their ability to completely receive what God is trying to do within them. God may be depositing His Word in them, however, they have taken action to prevent its implantation and growth. Complete intimacy and intercourse with God are inhibited. As a result, they are left unfruitful by their own choice.

Sexual intercourse for many has become less about "oneness" and procreation, and more about fun and pleasure. Please don't misunderstand—I am all about enjoying the pleasure of sex with my husband. I am not of the mindset that every sexual encounter with my husband should be to reproduce. With that said, sex is still an experience that is carelessly handled.

Few are in monogamous relationships. There are "hook up" sex, "quickie" sex, "adulterous" sex, "duty" sex, "abusive" sex, and "baby-making" sex to name a few. People can be with one partner today and another partner tomorrow. It is all about the "feel good" for many. This same thought process regarding intercourse has also infiltrated the church and affects the Kingdom of God consistently. I see believers having an encounter with God on Sunday, and "hooking up" with the devil on Monday. The relationship is not monogamous because you are rendezvousing with the enemy. Many times these extra-God affairs are kept secret to others, but God knows. The problem we have in the Kingdom of God is that many are so involved with the devil, that they have conceived his fruit from their idol worship (connectedness/intercourse). This is why I believe the kingdom of God is struggling with so much ungodliness, because many are birthing children of darkness instead of children of light right under our noses. As pastors and leaders in the church, we became so excited about the pregnancy itself, that we didn't take time to notice who the encounter was with. Even more concerning is the fact that we did not ask. We just assumed it was God.

> **MEN'S PERSPECTIVE**
>
>
>
> *Intercourse*
>
> I know that men and women have different views regarding sex. With that said, I don't know that I ever knew Greg's view regarding intercourse. Throughout our marriage, I know that I've asked him about his physical feelings during some of our sexual encounters, but I never asked him anything concerning his emotions and sex with me—until now.
>
> **Me:** *What is your purpose when engaging in intercourse with me as your wife?*
>
> **Greg:** *So the purpose in engaging in intercourse with you was for connection, intimacy, and pleasure.*

I am grateful for my hubby's honesty, yet his answer illuminated a revelation I could not ignore! Greg responded that his purpose for engaging in intercourse with me was for "connection, intimacy, and pleasure." I noticed that he never mentioned his purpose for engaging in intercourse with me was to reproduce. My initial thought was that this was such a typical male response. After all, the medical literature has demonstrated over the years that men and women view sex differently. Believe it or not, men need sex—it is a huge priority for them. In addition to their need for sex, men view sex mainly for physical gratification *(pleasure)*. On the contrary, sex for women is not often a high priority in a relationship. When they do engage in sex, they view it for emotional gratification *(love)*. For men—sex equates intimacy. For women, sex does not necessarily equate intimacy. Women define other activities such as talking regularly, social activities, nonsexual touching, etc., as intimacy. Neither view is good or bad; it's just different.

As I pondered Greg's answer, it became very clear to me that this male perspective of sex has influenced the way many of us engage in relationship with God. Think about it! Some of us engage with God when we want to feel good. Many times I have heard some say they go to church because they love the way it makes them feel. Or maybe that is *your* reason for going? You enjoy the good music, singing, and preaching. *Pleasure.* You enjoy the warm fellowship and family environment. *Intimacy.* Or maybe you've even expressed that you attend a specific church because you can relate to the pastor. *Connection.*

Similar to our natural relationships, God desires that in our intimate time with Him, we too experience pleasure. However, He does not want pleasure to be all we seek when engaging with Him. As women desire the intimate times of simply talking or spending time together with their husbands, God desires this same type of connection with us. Remember, it is through the spiritual intercourse of worship that God desires to deposit more of Himself and His Word into our hearts. If we are only seeking pleasure, we will miss the vital opportunities to receive the fullness of God.

Now, some of you may not have made a decision to fully commit to a relationship with God. Yet when tragedy occurs in your life, you are quick to call on God to make you *feel* better. If He is real enough to call on in times of need, then why isn't He real enough for you to fully engage in an intimate relationship with Him? *I'm just saying!* God does not want us to engage with Him for physical gratification only. Although He wants you to enjoy the hand-clapping, foot-stomping, and holy dancing experienced in His presence or at church, He wants to give you more. Who better knows how to grow what is inside you than the person who put it in you! Authentic intimacy and connection with God are the first steps to allowing Him to activate all the greatness He has placed in you.

FOUR

The Deposit

FERTILIZATION & CONCEPTION

To conceive or not to conceive, that is the question! Conception results from the uniting of seeds. Everything produced in this world began as a simple seed: the seed of an idea, the seed of a fruit, seed money, and of course the seed of a male and female. When the seed of a man unites with the ovum of a woman, new life is produced! Spiritual conception operates no differently than nature's way of producing. You need a seed. Christ is The Seed. Believers must possess a mature seed of faith that can unite with Christ and produce new spiritual life. To Conceive or Not to Conceive? Spiritually, that is determined by you!

In obstetrics, regular ovulation and intercourse alone, are not enough for pregnancy to take place. There is much more to this process that leads to a pregnancy. Once the egg is released from the ovary, it must be fertilized by the seed of the male partner in order for pregnancy to even have a chance to develop. As we've already discussed, intercourse is the joining together of two individuals sexually. This joining together involves penetration. Penetration is merely "the insertion" of a male's genitalia into that of a woman. Penetration is the initiation of intercourse. Despite the importance of intercourse to conception, there are many that start the act of intercourse, but do not finish it. In other words, *completed* intercourse did not happen. Intercourse is defined as completed if "semen passes from the male into the female body" (Merriam Webster). What makes it completed is that a deposit occurred. You see, some engage in intercourse but stop short of arousal, orgasm or ejaculation. It is during the peak of the male orgasm that ejaculation takes place moving sperm from the testes, through the penis, and finally, depositing into the female's vaginal canal. Ejaculation is the completed, God designed purpose of intercourse.

Failing to complete intercourse means there is no sperm deposit or ejaculate released. Without this sperm deposit, pregnancy has NO chance of occurring. Just like completed intercourse, "completed worship" should end in a deposit being made. Now remember, in the last chapter, we discussed the spiritual parallel between intercourse and worship. At this moment, I don't want to focus merely on worship, but the necessity of "completed worship." Anything short of this, is not total worship. It may feel good and bring pleasure, but will produce no fruit.

Similar to the natural, many believers engage in worship with the Lord. However, right when the Lord is about to make a divine deposit from Himself into the believer, he or she stops worshipping. I've often seen this in church on multiple occasions. I've watched the power of the Holy Spirit move greatly over individuals while they were worshipping, and as a result, they experienced the inability to control their emotions or behavior (crying, jumping, raising hands, etc.). As the Holy Spirit continued to move upon them, they became fearful of what they were experiencing and abruptly stopped worshiping. This fear may be due to embarrassment of others watching, losing control, or the fear of the unknown. Sometimes it is not fear, but simply pride. Other times it is nothing more than, distraction. Think about it, have you ever been in the middle of worshiping at home and the phone rings, the baby cries, or you remember something you were supposed to do? Whatever the reason, completed worship does not take place and as a result, a deposit from the Lord is often not received. Identical to the natural, no spiritual pregnancy can or will occur from that encounter.

Push Vitamin

Completed worship is important. Eliminate distraction during your worship with God.

Throughout the Bible, you will find multiple verses stating, "... he knew her, and she conceived." Notice that the act of knowing (intercourse) when demonstrated in the Bible, ordinarily resulted in one conceiving. Intercourse was expected to lead to conception, and when it didn't, it was devastating to those that suffered with barrenness. Many women engage in sexual intercourse hoping to get pregnant. Medically speaking, they are hoping for fertilization and implantation. Fertilization is imperative to the process of pregnancy, but what does fertilization really mean in the process of pregnancy?

The fertilization process is defined by the uniting of the male sperm with the female egg (the ovum). It is at this point that the development of new life begins. I must say, I never realized WHAT a sperm has to endure in order to fertilize a human egg! Oh my goodness, talk about a dangerous journey filled with attacks, rejection, and death. *Humm! Sounds like a journey someone else took more than 2000 years ago.*

So let's look further at what happens after a sperm deposit is made. I'm going to take you back to Health Class 101. Remember, I told you that the journey of the sperm to the egg is quite treacherous and risky! Although only one sperm is needed to fertilize the mature egg; anywhere between 20 - 500 million sperm are ejaculated into the woman's vagina during a single episode of sexual intercourse. Although that is a lot of sperm, the problem is that they're being deposited into an extremely harsh environment for sperm survival. You see, the pH balance of the vagina is normally acidic in order to prevent various bacteria, viruses, and fungi from causing vaginal and cervical infection. Although this is good for infection prevention, it is detrimental to sperm, which have great difficulty living in acidic conditions. In fact, research has demonstrated that the majority of the sperm released, die just a few hours after being deposited within the vagina.

Now, for those sperms that make it further, their fight for survival and travel to the released mature egg continues to be one of exceptional challenge. From the vagina, the sperms must navigate their way into the narrow opening of the cervix in hopes of making it into the uterine cavity. In the course of doing so, millions of more sperms are killed due to being trapped in the thick, sticky cervical mucus. Once in the uterine cavity, the remaining sperms strive to reach their final destination of the fallopian tube where the mature egg awaits. The sperm casualty, at this point, exceeds into the millions, leaving only thousands to make the final leg of the journey. Surviving sperms continue to follow chemical and thermo signals that are said to be released from the awaiting egg. These signals are how the sperm knows the direction to travel, in order to find the mature egg.

Once inside the fallopian tube it is a race for one sperm to penetrate the egg and get to its inner aspect. Penetration, however, is not an easy task for any sperm. *Why?* Well, just like we place protective walls up emotionally, to keep others from getting in, so does a woman's egg. Imagine trying to break through something (or someone) that seemingly doesn't want to let anything in? In case you haven't caught the medical-spiritual parallelism yet, here it is.

We know that the Seed of God is the Word. We know that the Word of God, is Christ. Therefore the Seed of God, is Christ. Medically speaking, we know the seed of a male is his sperm. As already mentioned, these seeds are moved from the safe environment of the male testicles, into the harsh environment of the vaginal canal during ejaculation. In comparison, The Seed of God, Christ Jesus, was moved from His habitation of Heaven to the harsh environment of our earth to reconcile man back to God. Jesus Christ, came to seek those that would accept Him. However, it was not an easy mission. Once He arrived on earth, His life *(like that of the male seed - sperm)* was filled with attacks, rejection, and death. Yet and still, He continued to push forward in pursuit of those He was sent to save and birth new life. It is our faith that He is drawn towards.

Like sperm, which follow the signal being released by the mature egg; Jesus is following the signal being released by our mature faith. Just like the mature egg releases a substance (hormone) that activates the brain, so does our maturing faith release a substance that activates the movement of Christ more towards us. That is how our Lord Jesus Christ finds us! Wow! Who would have ever thought that there would be such parallel between sperm (as man's natural seed) and Christ, as our Spiritual Seed? Well, there is more!

Back to the medical. Penetration is not easy for any sperm. *That's where we left off.* To understand the process of penetration, we must talk about the structure of the mature egg a little further. Throughout the entire development of the mature egg, an outer membrane or covering, called the *zona pellucida,* has encapsulated it and serves as a protective barrier while it was developing inside the ovary. This covering remains wrapped around the mature egg after its release. The *zona pellucida* is tough and does not give itself over easy to allowing a sperm to get through its barrier.

What's interesting is that once a sperm has arrived to where the mature egg is waiting, it binds to this outer shell. However, attaching itself to the *zona pellucida* is not enough. Penetration does not automatically and immediately occur upon binding alone. In order for the attached sperm to penetrate the egg, the sperm must begin to go through a chemical change (acrosome reaction). This chemical change causes the sperm to release special substances which break down the outer membrane of the egg, allowing the attached sperm to now penetrate the egg.

Once the sperm has penetrated the egg, the *zona pellucida* begins to release a signal that drives other sperms back from the egg. This serves to prevent multiple penetrations from other sperms. Fertilization has finally occurred, but this is only the beginning.

Now, back to the spiritual! I see many people praying to God and seeking Him for new life, new direction, and new hope. Like the male seed (sperm), The Seed (the Word of God) arrives to where our faith (small yet matured) has led Him. The problem however, is that He arrives to find that we have placed a spiritual *zona pellucida* around our hearts. As a result, many of us (like the awaiting egg), make it very difficult for Jesus Christ to enter our lives and create new life. We have put up barriers to keep others out, including Him. We have fortified the barriers around our

Many of us make it very difficult for Jesus Christ to enter our lives and create new life. We have put up barriers to keep others out, including Him.

hearts, our spirits, and our minds. We make Jesus Christ, work so hard for us to accept His Word. As a result of the many barriers around man's heart, countless remain the same old creatures despite multiple encounters with the Lord.

Interestingly enough, *zona pellucida,* in Latin, means "the zone of transparency." Transparency, as we all know, indicates that something is clear or that it is of a quality that it can be seen through. It also means "openness." Spiritually speaking, numerous believers all over the world are unable to become pregnant with the things of God simply because their transparency is not open to God or themselves. They are afraid to completely open themselves up to God. As a result, their seed of faith, though waiting, is unable to be fertilized by the Seed of Christ (the Word). Sadly, when this continues in the life of a believer, a time for pushing can never occur. However, when we, as the children of God yield ourselves to openness, the Seed of God can enter in. Once in, transformation can now take place as new life is divinely created.

Transformation. This takes place in the final stages of human fertilization. Once the sperm has penetrated the egg, the two fuse together and an exchange between genetic material begins to take place. *I just thought about the scripture, Mark 10:8, which says, "The two shall become one..." This not only occurs spiritually, but also biologically. The sperm and the ovum fuse together to become one entity. The transformation resulting from this fusion will ultimately develop into one new creature.*

Okay back to transformation. The fertilized egg is now called a zygote. This is a one-cell embryo. The sperm has been nothing more than a carrier of the genetic material of the father, *just like the Seed of Christ, who is the genetic material of The Father.* The same is true for the egg, except that it contains the genetic material of the mother. This genetic material consists of everything needed to determine every characteristic and trait of the new baby that will develop. Everything from personality, color of skin and eyes, talents, etc., is already determined. The process must still take place but the outcome is already determined.

 **TAKE A LOOK INSIDE:**

Transformation. How Does It Look?

Once fertilization takes place the maternal egg and the sperm fuse together. The sperm and ovum both release their genetic make-up. A new one-celled organism forms and is the early embryo in its primitive form, called a zygote.

The zygote now undergoes a process called cleavage. Cleavage is the process in which rapid cell division occurs, transforming the one-celled embryo into a solid ball containing hundreds of cells. This is called a blastula, which will later rearrange the cells and become a structure called a blastocyst. This blastocyst is what will later implant inside the uterine cavity. It contains an inner mass of cells which will develop into the baby, and an outer layer of cells which will become the placenta.

My God! That reminds me of the fact that once Christ comes into our lives, we are complete. He has placed everything in us (His spiritual DNA) that will determine what we shall be! We just simply go through the process although our victorious outcome has already been determined. We must simply allow our faith to fuse with His Word so that we can develop into what He has already determined we would be over 2000 years ago. Our only responsibility is to let the Word *abide in us, and us in Him.* We must implant the word of God in our hearts so that we can become living "epistles." This means that we will be the image of Christ (the Word) in the earth (Romans 8:28-30). As we develop as the new creatures in Christ, so does our discovery of the greatness, the purpose, the hopes and the dreams that He predestined us to manifest.

Once the genetic material of both the mature egg and sperm are released, a new cell structure develops and continues to transform. The conception of new life has begun and the "new creature," in its early development, is guided further through the fallopian tube, towards the uterus, where it will then implant underneath the lining of the uterus.

Likewise, the fertilization of your faith by the Word of God (Jesus Christ), should lead to a uniting of your spirit with the Spirit of Christ. This fusion should lead to a spiritual transformation within you, the believer, as the DNA of Christ is released and joined with your DNA, producing new life (a conceptus). This Word of God, that has created new life, should be implanted in the deeper parts of our hearts, so that it can multiply and grow to where it will eventually be manifested externally upon its birth.

MEN'S PERSPECTIVE

Making the Deposit

When a man has a release (ejaculation) during sex with his wife, he has completed intercourse, resulting in a deposit of millions of seeds into her most intimate parts. Without the release of seeds, there is no potential to reproduce. In over two decades of marriage Greg and I have had the pleasure of sharing many releases together. Three of which resulted in the reproduction of three beautiful gifts named Brooke, Morgan, & Caleb. I asked Greg for insight regarding his view of release during our sexual encounters.

Me: *How did you view our sexual encounter when you had a release versus no release during our love-making?*

Greg: *Release represented complete satisfaction, and the completing of the design of men – emptying out; giving it all.*

Me: *What about times you did not ejaculate because we had to stop suddenly, or something else prevented you from doing so?*

Greg: *Usually, I was in pain the rest of the day. Because I was full, and didn't get a release.*

Satisfaction. I imagined that my husband, like most men, experienced great pleasure during the release phase of our intercourse. However, when he expressed that making a deposit brought him "complete satisfaction," I realized my need to ensure that during our sexual encounters, I take time for him to have this experience. Moreover, I was challenged with the reality that I am not often concerned with a deposit being made. As a woman, my satisfaction is complete when I experience the pleasure I desire to receive.

The reality is that many of us have this mindset towards God. Like most men, I believe God receives complete satisfaction when He is able to make a deposit and fully empty out of Himself what He has been holding specifically for each of us. The problem is that many of us are so focused on the pleasures we desire to receive, that we often don't make time for God to release what He has for us. Commonly, there are things that prevent or distract us right at the critical time God desires to make a deposit into our spirit and lives. On the other hand, some of us may not make time for God to release what He has for us because we honestly don't want to reproduce anything at that time. Our desire to avoid reproducing often isn't because we don't love God, but because we don't want to produce anything we would ultimately have to be responsible for.

In the field of gynecology, we recognize that some individuals practice the method of "withdrawal" to prevent pregnancy. This method of birth control involves the male withdrawing his penis from the female at the time he starts ejaculating, in order to prevent his seed (sperm) from uniting with the woman's ovum. In reality, many of you are utilizing this same practice in your relationships with God. You develop connectedness and intimacy with God, but then you withdraw before a deposit can be made by Him into your spirit. You avoid fertilization of what God has placed in you by His Word. You want to have a relationship, but often do not want to commit to the responsibilities that often come with it. As a result, I believe God is hurt by many of our decisions to only seek to enjoy the pleasure of

Him but, not to desire to reproduce His image in the earth.

Pain. I learned early on in my marriage the consequences of my hubby becoming full of seeds yet unable to release them. You see, when men are reaching the excitation phase of their sexual response, the blood vessels in the testicles and penis become engorged with blood. This engorgement results from an increased amount of blood filling and becoming trapped within the man's genitalia. Additionally, this engorgement causes the testicles to become enlarged and the penis to erect during the arousal state. Once ejaculation occurs, the blood in the testicles decrease and its flow returns to normal. When a release does not occur and a deposit is not made, the increased blood remains trapped within the testicles causing achiness, pain, or heaviness.

Heaviness and achiness of heart are what I believe God feels when He is unable to release the wonderful deposits into our lives that He has purposed for us. His pain arises from His disappointment of being full yet unable to release. Men were designed to deposit. Think about it. The sexual organs of women are designed to receive, while the sexual organs of a man are designed to deposit into something. God has so much He desires to deposit into our lives if we would only commit to a deeper relationship with Him.

I was genuinely enlightened when Greg stated his full sense of feeling that he was "completing the design of men by giving it all." Personally, I would have never associated men making a deposit during intercourse with fulfilling the purpose of their design. Nevertheless, it's true! Men get great satisfaction in releasing during intercourse because it is what they were designed to do! Likewise, since man was made in the image of God, God is simply fulfilling the purpose of His design when He makes deposits into us. Whether deposits of healing, faith, love, wisdom, skill, knowledge, peace, hope, greatness, and so on—He is manifesting to us Who He is and what He has purposed Himself to be in our lives.

As our spiritual Father, God gets great satisfaction when He is able to fully release (deposit) what He has for you to you. It is who He is by design. The reality is that if you choose not to allow the seed of God to fertilize what He has already placed in you, then you risk uniting with someone or something else that will likely produce something other than the fullness of what God intended for you to birth. When this occurs, the quality of what is produced is often compromised.

Five

The Attachment

IMPLANTATION

Down, down, down through the fallopian tube the embryo travels towards the uterine cavity. Although invisible to those looking at the outward body, a massive change is nevertheless occurring on the inside. The one-celled embryo is rapidly multiplying into hundreds of cells. In addition to the change that is occurring within the newly developing embryo, movement is also taking place as it continues its journey towards the uterine cavity. Transformation requires movement – both invisible and visible. In life, good transformation will cause movement away from negative people, behavior, or thinking; and towards an environment whereby you can take root to positively grow and develop. The question is: "Are you willing to change?" Some of us are not willing to allow God to transform our minds and our thinking. As a result, we are unable to arrive at the predestined place where He has chosen for us to ultimately grow and develop. For this reason, many spiritual abortions

> *take place because His Word for our lives is unable to implant within our hearts.*

After fertilization of the mature egg occurs, transformation begins. Magnificent change and development are taking place with the protection of the *zona pellucida,* which still serves as the protective shell around the developing embryo. Spiritually speaking, faith is the outer shield that serves to protect what God is doing inside of us. Like the male seed that penetrates the mature egg, Christ the Seed penetrates and works in and through our mature faith. It is our mature faith that often sustains the work that God is doing in each of us.

The zona pellucida functions as the outer shell of the mature egg, which keeps unwanted things out. This role is extremely important since the inside of the mature egg contains the precious substance of new life, which must be protected as it grows. Faith is no different. We have already revealed the parallel between mature faith and the mature egg. Mature faith contains "the substance of things hoped for and the evidence of things not seen" (Hebrews 11:1, KJV). The outer shell of our faith (the spiritual zona pellucida) serves to keep things out that could compromise our hopes and beliefs while our faith continues to increase inside of us. Your uncompromised hopes and beliefs are essential to your ability to one day manifest the greatness, purpose, hopes, and dreams that lie within you.

Commit this to your memory: *the role and function of faith is to shield!* Confirmation of this is seen in the Word of God where the "shield of faith" is discussed as a part of the armor of God that we, as believers, are instructed to "put on." Specifically, we are instructed "in all circumstances," take up the shield of faith with which you can extinguish all the flaming darts of the evil one" (Ephesians 6:16, ESV). Faith is essential to believing that God will complete in us what He has promised.

Now, let's get back to the medical. We were talking about the transformation of the embryonic cells while being protected within the confines of the *zona pellucida*. Although these changes are occurring, at this point, the primary goal of this post fertilization process is multiplication of the embryonic cells and their relocation from the inside of the fallopian tube to the uterine cavity where it will be implanted. If you were looking under a microscope during this phase of transformation, you would see multiple cells rapidly dividing and increasing in number. *The one-cell embryo has divided into a two-celled structure. That two-celled structure divided into a four-celled structure, then a six-celled structure, an eight-celled structure, and so on.* At this stage, these cells are identical. There is no difference. Their role and function have not yet been revealed. In fact, they all look the same and function the same.

Once the embryonic cells enter the uterine cavity, the cells begin to rearrange themselves from a solid ball of cells into a hollow ball, forming what is called a blastocyst. More specifically, the blastocyst is the transformation of the embryo from a solid mass of cells into a fluid filled ball surrounded by a single layer of cells. Within the fluid filled ball of cells is a small solid mass of cells. During this phase of rearrangement, the cells of the embryonic structure begin to reveal their future function. *Remember I told you earlier all the cells look and function the same.* In medicine, we call this "differentiation," meaning that the cells become "different" or distinct from one another. They no longer function the same and look the same; their cellular identity becomes clear and distinct. As a result, the inner mass of cells inside of the fluid filled ball, will become the developing baby. The outer layer of cells will eventually become the placenta, which will provide nourishment to the growing fetus.

Oh my! I got to stop here and discuss the spiritual revelation that parallels so closely with this post fertilization phase of the process. We have already determined that it is mature faith that must be fertilized by the Word of God (Christ) in order for the process, leading towards spiritual pregnancy, to begin. Once faith is fertilized by the Word of God, together they begin to multiply and cause transformation to begin in the life of the believer. Through the power of the Holy Spirit, Christ begins to rearrange our thinking, our behavior, and the way we use to function. The way our old self used to function becomes reorganized into the new person we are becoming through the Word of God by

Push Vitamin

Through the power of the Holy Spirit, Christ begins to rearrange our thinking, our behavior, and the way we use to function.

Submit to the process and be transformed!

faith.

As new believers, we become "differentiated," or *different* from the world. Our function or purpose in life becomes identified and distinct. In the early stages, this transformation although rapid is unable to be seen externally. It is a divinely internal process, which is actively bringing about a change that cannot yet be visualized. This change is actively transforming us into a new person (embryo) that will one day be manifested. *Or will it?*

Okay. Before we answer that question, we have to go back to the medical. Stay with me for a moment while I lay the foundation to understanding the next medical spiritual parallel.

Now, approximately seven days after ovulation, the newly formed embryo reaches the uterus and is ready to be implanted. This will be the commencement of pregnancy. In preparation of the implantation process, the embryo, like a baby chicken, is ready to enter the world and begins to hatch from the *zona pellucida*. Once hatched, it will begin to rotate slowly across the lining of the uterus to an area where it will ultimately attach.

When a strong attachment has occurred, the embryo begins to bury itself underneath the lining of the uterus, where the luscious blood supply is awaiting its receipt. *Remember, the blood supply to the uterine lining has been increasing throughout the woman's menstrual cycle in preparation for an anticipated pregnancy.* It is ready and prepared to provide the necessary environment for growth and development of the new creation. Upon the completion of implantation, the pregnancy hormone is now secreted into the urine and blood stream. Pregnancy has successfully taken place and can now be verified.

In the field of obstetrics, implantation of the embryo *is* the definition of pregnancy. One can only be called pregnant if what was fertilized has now been implanted. Leading up to this point, the process of becoming pregnant has been occurring. However pregnancy has not been established until the embryo has penetrated and buried itself underneath the uterine lining. In preparation for writing this chapter, I learned that the attachment phase of implantation is extremely important. In fact, defects in the attachment stage of implantation are a common cause for infertility. The embryo must have a strong adherence to the uterine lining if implantation is going to be successful.

Interestingly enough, I also discovered that the ability of the embryo to attach to the uterine lining largely relies upon what's called "uterine receptivity." Surprisingly, uterine receptivity, as it pertains to implantation, is only available between days 20-24 of a woman's menstrual cycle. If implantation of the embryo does not occur within this window of time, pregnancy will not occur. This reminds me of the importance of timing. I don't ever want to miss what God desires for me because I wasn't "receptive" at the time He was ready to make a deposit or place His gift in me.

As a general OB/Gyn, my area of expertise does not require me to have an extensive knowledge of the complex biochemistry components involved in pregnancy. As a result, I have gladly avoided its nuances. *Oh! How I hated chemistry and biochemistry in medical school!* Yet, I found it quite intriguing and such a powerful revelation when I began studying the process of implantation. As a result, I think it necessary to discuss the basics of the implantation process.

Implantation begins with attachment of the embryo to the uterine lining, which sounds simple enough; however, there is more. So, let's look at the implantation process much closer. According to the *Oxford Journal*, human embryo implantation is a three-stage process (apposition, adhesion and invasion) involving synchronized crosstalk between a receptive endometrium and a functional blastocyst (Human Reproductive Update (November/December 2006) 12 (6): 731-746). This means that communication signals are occurring between the uterine lining and the early embryo.

So let me stop here for a moment. I want you to understand that implantation involves communication, whether natural or spiritual. Just like communication signals between the embryo and the endometrial lining are required, so too is communication between us and God necessary for His Word and purpose to be implanted in us.

As I mentioned previously, the beginning of pregnancy begins with implantation. However, as we see here, the process of

> ...*communication between us and God is necessary for His Word and purpose to be implanted in us.*

implantation involves three phases. Oh my goodness! I feel the spiritual revelation coming forth! But first, let me define each phase of this process.

Apposition is the first phase of implantation. This phase involves the attachment of the embryo to the uterine lining once it enters the cavity. Although attachment has taken place, it is loose, and as a result, the embryonic structure is not fixed in its place. It's a weak connection that can easily be detached. The second phase of implantation is Adhesion. In this phase, the loosely attached embryo now becomes strongly adhered to the endometrial lining. The attachment is strong and fixed. It's unmovable.

Finally, the third phase of implantation is **Invasion**. At this point, the embryo now penetrates and invades the deeper layer of the uterine lining. Once buried, it begins to take root, grow and develop into a fetus. That is of course, if the implantation takes place within the window of "uterine receptivity" previously mentioned. It's a short period, and what's even more amazing is the fact that successful implantation requires more than just a receptive endometrium. As previously mentioned, "a normal and functional embryo at the blastocyst developmental stage and a synchronized dialogue between maternal and embryonic tissues" (Hum. Reprod. Update, September 2006) are also necessary.

Many in the Kingdom of God are not only full of faith, but they are releasing this faith consistently. Their problem is not that they aren't yet spiritually fertile. Instead, it's that once they release faith, and this faith unites with God's Word, it subsequently goes no further. Yes, the Word begins to cause early changes and transformation within the individual, but pregnancy never takes place because the believer fails to allow the new creature (spiritual embryo) he or she is becoming to undergo implantation.

In obstetrics, we call this a *chemical pregnancy*. It's when a mature egg is fertilized and yet unable to implant completely, resulting in a positive pregnancy test and a pregnancy that never develops. Remember, the embryonic tissue must be implanted in the lining of the uterus where the rich and abundant blood flow is present and where the embryo can take root and begin to develop into a fully formed baby. Many times this inability to implant results from the fact that the environment within the uterine cavity is not right. There may be infections, fibroid tumors, polyps, anatomical anomalies, or other things present that inhibit the attachment of the early embryo.

Similarly, *fertilized faith* that has now fused with the Word of God, must be implanted in the heart of the believer. It is one thing to release mature faith; it is another thing to maintain it. Sometimes you may have the right faith but you're in the wrong environment for your faith to grow and develop. Sadly, pregnancy is compromised.

Ephesians 3:17 says, "That Christ may dwell in your hearts through faith..." This scripture provides evidence, and supports the medical-spiritual parallel concerning faith being fertilized by the word of God and then implanted in the heart of man. The Bible also says, "thy word have I hid in my heart that I might not sin against thee" (Psalm 119:11). To hide the word in your heart means the same thing as to implant or bury. Finally, James 1:21 instructs us to "...receive with meekness the engrafted word which is able to save your souls." The word "engraft" is derived from the word "graft."

In medicine, the word "graft" often refers to the relocation of tissue or an organ from another source internally or externally from the patient. It often denotes transplanted or implanted tissue. Moreover, when tissue is grafted into the body of a patient, it simply means it was inserted and attached to other tissue. The engrafted tissue becomes a permanently attached part of the individual's body. It is fixed!

James 1:21, reveals this very same medical concept. Once the Word of God has been inserted into our hearts, we must "receive" it with meekness. *Hmmm. Could it be that the spiritual "window of receptivity" includes meekness?* Once received with meekness, the Word of God can now undergo the process of Implantation. As a result, the received Word of God (apposition) will become permanently attached (adhesion) to the heart of the believer (invasion). Once "adhesed," the Word of God will now invade deeper into the heart of the believer where the blood of Jesus will continue to cover and supply everything needed for him or her to develop into the new creature He purposed.

Unfortunately, many in the Kingdom of God fail to experience implantation. In medicine, studies reveal that over half of fertilized eggs fail to implant, which results in implantation defects being a common cause of infertility in women. Sometimes this can be due to the fact that the developing embryo is not healthy or able to function correctly. Other times it can be due to the fact that the atmosphere is not conducive to implantation. As it is in the natural, so it is in the spiritual. Mature faith can be fertilized by the Word of God but fail to implant in the heart where growth and development takes place. This failure to implant can be due to a malfunction in any one of the phases of implantation. For example, many believers hear the Word of God and loosely attach their faith to it (apposition). This creates wavering faith. A faith that is easily movable or detached. A faith that often dissipates when difficult times arise.

It is essential that faith, like the human embryo, become strongly adhered in the heart of the believer (Adhesion). This allows the new creature being developed to become steadfast and unmovable in the Lord. Moreover, this individual is secure and fixed in the things of God. Finally, the developing believer must allow the Word of God to invade his/her heart. When this occurs the Word of God becomes engrafted in you, thus allowing yourself to be rooted, grounded, and established in the things of God (Ephesians 3:17-22, NKJV).

Finally, we must understand the importance of preparing our hearts to receive the Word of God. The state of our heart greatly affects our ability to become impregnated with the things of God. Just like the uterus has a "receptivity window," so too do the hearts of men. Many times the Word of God is attempting to penetrate deeper into our hearts; however, we have allowed our hearts to become hardened or even broken by various circumstances of life. This results in the heart's inability to be "receptive to the Word of God."

Other times, as the Book of James reveals, our hearts are not in a state of meekness, which is why he felt led to instruct the believer to "receive with meekness" (1:21). When our hearts are not meek, we will not yield to, submit to, or obey the Word of God. Consequently, the implantation of God's Word by faith does not happen, resulting in no pregnancy. Once you allow the Word of God by faith to implant in your heart: you are now spiritually pregnant and ready to develop into the fullness of who God predestined you to be.

SIX

The Pregnancy

GROWTH & DEVELOPMENT

Two weeks after my confirmation of pregnancy appointment, at which time the serum pregnancy test was positive and my proof of pregnancy was established, I now return for my initial OB visit. Yes!

Identical to the last visit, I am sitting in the exam room awaiting the entrance of the doctor. Today I am clothed with the infamous blue office gown, and once again, the common white sheet is draped across my legs. I am fully naked, yet I understand the purpose of today's visit is to receive a full physical examination and evaluation of my medical history. I will be exposed. Finally, the obstetrician enters the room and the detailed history taking begins.

A ll of us have purpose and greatness in us! In fact, it's been in us our whole lives just waiting for us to recognize it! Perhaps you or someone else have already confirmed the greatness and purpose that lies within you. Perhaps you are still searching. When we accept God into our hearts, a wonderful transformation not only occurs in our character, behavior and personality, but also in our spirit.

When we decide to be in an authentic relationship with God, then we allow Him to grow us in every area of our lives: spiritually, emotionally, and physically. Although God doesn't need a church to grow and develop us, we need the church to help us understand the growth and development that will begin to take place in our lives. Additionally, we need someone to ensure that we are developing appropriately. Think about it from a natural perspective. That's why women need obstetricians.

The journey of pregnancy in women involves physical and emotional changes that can be seen externally; as well as, physiological changes that are taking place within the developing fetus internally. Similarly, the journey of spiritual pregnancy in all of us involves changes that occur in our attitude, character, thinking, and emotions.

As we begin to undergo these changes within ourselves, it now gives rise to the growth and development of our greatness, purpose, hopes, and dreams that lie within us. Even more so, we become aware of what these things specifically are (books, businesses, ministry, professional or academic dreams, or other platforms and endeavors) that will be birthed. To ensure the optimal health of what is going to be delivered, a woman needs an obstetrician to manage her developmental course through prenatal visits. You need church and God to manage your spiritual pregnancy course through attending a Christ-led church, complete with Bible study, prayer, and fellowship.

In obstetrics, the initial prenatal visit (PNV) is all about identifying risk factors that can compromise the pregnancy. The questions investigate for risks that may originate directly from the mom-to-be. The inspection for high blood pressure, diabetes, history of preterm labor, risky behavior, and other medical conditions are pursued intentionally. A detailed pursuit is imperative so that the need for early intervention and management can be determined. Likewise, a similar inspection is also performed to seek out pregnancy risks exhibited directly from the fetus. Are there risks for chromosomal abnormalities, fetal defects, or the like? How old is the fetus, when is the Expected Date of Delivery (EDD)? All these questions are important because they identify risks that can compromise the health of the pregnancy.

After the history-taking, the examination begins. The heart, lungs, neck, and abdomen are examined, as commonly done in a general exam. The examination however, does not stop there due to the obstetrical and gynecological nature of the visit. Her more intimate body parts are exposed and examined—the breast, and finally her genitalia. The exam usually ends with an internal pelvic exam being performed. This is an intimate exam which, for some, may be uncomfortable and feel awkward. Nevertheless, it is necessary and should not be avoided. To avoid it could lead to the potential to miss the ability to diagnose active infections and/or reproductive organ pathology that could later compromise the outcome of the pregnancy.

I believe this same type of examination needs to take place in the life of the believers who have just discovered that God has impregnated them with His Word. Unfortunately, some churches seem to overlook the need to initially examine all those who announce they are spiritually pregnant. As a result, some become frustrated with their inability to push out purpose, hopes or dreams at a time they predetermined.

Since confirmation of their pregnancy was never determined, they wasted time and energy pushing when pregnant they were not! Others have been confirmed, but never returned for spiritual care. As a result, they struggle to develop appropriate behavior, character, and/or pregnancy course. Additionally, they may birth gifts that are malformed or premature, which ultimately are unable to function or give abundant life. How do they know they are pregnant? Who has confirmed it? Even more importantly, who has performed the initial spiritual exam? We will talk more about this very thing later in the chapter.

Similar to the medical, a newly pregnant child of God needs to be assessed to determine if there is anything within him or her that could compromise the new creature God is creating him/her to be. Can your current lifestyle compromise what God is spiritually doing internally? Deep and intimate questions may need to be asked to investigate all areas within your life that could have the potential to compromise the spiritual pregnancy. Yes, I understand that this kind of exposure can cause you to feel uncomfortable or even awkward; however, the truth remains that the intricacies of risks must still be pursued with love, honesty and compassion. Failing to do so could result in the compromise or death of what God is developing in you specifically as a new creature in Him. Additionally, it could also compromise the purpose or greatness He is developing within you.

At times during the pregnancy, the opportunity to test for genetic concerns are offered to the patient, to ensure the fetus is normal and without chromosomal defects. Likewise, this is not a bad idea to also test the genetic make-up of some of the spiritual pregnancies taking place in the Kingdom of God. Why? Because the reality is that not everyone is pregnant with the things of God. In fact, some have been sleeping with the enemy! As I mentioned, previously in the book, some are having "extra-God" affairs. Not everyone in church is being faithful in his or her relationship with God. Many more times than I would like to admit, some individuals were not fertilized by the Word of God but the seed of the enemy. As a result, they are pregnant and the pregnancy often fails to birth the image of God. Although testing while pregnant cannot determine who the father is, it can indicate whether the genetic make-up is normal or abnormal. The only way to know early on and before birth is to test for it.

Pregnancy/ Prenatal Care

Life of a new creature commences at fertilization when the sperm and egg unite. Pregnancy, as we discussed earlier, starts with implantation and is all about the process of life that has been developing internally. More specifically, pregnancy is all about that invisible process becoming visible and evident. It provides evidence that something is truly growing and developing inside of a woman's body. That something is a "new creature."

The anticipated goal of pregnancy is to deliver a viable, healthy, and mature fetus. As an obstetrician, my role and purpose is to monitor and manage this process of pregnancy. I monitor the growth and development of the fetus and manage conditions that may arise and have the potential to compromise the health of mom and baby. Remember, the anticipated goal is to bring a healthy baby to full term—maturity. As a result, the focus of prenatal care is to provide regularly, scheduled appointments to closely monitor the pregnancy process and intervene when necessary. Pregnancy is divided into trimesters. These trimesters represent a three-month period within a pregnancy. The focus of each trimester will be different. Likewise, the clinical management for each trimester will also be different. Throughout the remainder of this chapter, we will discuss the focus of each trimester and its parallel to spiritual pregnancy.

The First Trimester

Differentiation & Development. The first trimester consists of weeks 1-12 of the pregnancy. During this time, differentiation and development take place within the newly developing creature. Differentiation is "the action or process of differentiating" (online dictionary). More simply put, it is the process of becoming different. Remember, we discussed that after fertilization takes place the cells begin to divide and multiply—forming a ball of cells. If you recall, I told you these cells all look the same and function the same. What type of cells they shall become has not yet been revealed. They are identical. At this point, there is no difference.

Now, after the embryo reaches the uterus, the cells begin to lose their sameness and become distinct. They begin to develop their specialized function. The purpose of each cell begins to unfold. Similarly, the believer who is in this same stage of pregnancy spiritually begins to be made aware of his or her specific function and purpose in life. This unfolding, regarding the depths of his or her gifts, is often revealed by God Himself through prayer and worship. We become differentiated.

This is the time that you may begin to realize your purpose on earth and why God created you! The specifics and the details of your purpose may not always be clear, however the generalities of it may be. For example, you may realize that your purpose is to help people; however, the specifics of how you will do that may not yet be clear, and gaining that clarity will come as you mature. Maturity requires time and support, which we will discuss later in this chapter.

As the process of cell differentiation continues, the cells begin to develop into specific tissue and organs within the developing fetus. After a while, a process that was invisible to the naked eye develops into something visible: a tiny new creature. This same process will take place in the believers as we continue to grow with God. The specifics of our specialized functions will be revealed completely. As we grow in Christ and begin to move into our purpose, our invisible transformation in God becomes visible to the eyes of others.

By the end of the first eight weeks of pregnancy, the newly developing creature is no longer an embryo but has now become a fetus. *What's the difference?* Well, remember that the embryonic stage of development is all about cells "differentiating" and beginning to assume different functions. What was once a ball of unspecified cells has now developed into specific and different types of cells: brain, bone, skin, stomach, heart, and legs. Once all the various types of cells needed to develop into a complete human being are present, the embryo is now called a fetus.

Spiritually, this is about the time you start to feel God leading you towards a specific type of ministry or gifting within the Body of Christ, which is the church. You may feel led to join the children's ministry or become a praise dancer. You may feel led to invest your time helping others that are struggling financially, or socioeconomically. You may feel led to go back to school to teach, or start a specific business that will fill a need within your community.

These desires and "senses of purpose" are resulting from the fact that you have spiritually grown from a spiritual embryo to a fetus.

Medically, the development in the fetal phase is classified as the growth and development phase. I like to call it the "manifestation and growth" stage. I think of it this way: at this point, every cell needed for this new creature (fetus) to develop is already present. Now only *time* is needed for these cells to continue to develop and manifest visibly what they were always destined to be. Therefore, what was once a group of brain cells will now transform into a visible brain. This visible brain, although small, is now manifested. Growth and maturity of the brain, or any other fetal tissues, are what transpire in the second and third trimester.

Likewise, the same process occurs after one's heart has been fertilized by the Word of God. After the Word of God penetrates the heart of an individual, he or she becomes different. Behavior, thinking, and talking should become distinctly different from the original worldly behavior. One's function in the Body of Christ begins to develop and over time, it will visibly manifest who each individual is destined to be. It's interesting that cell differentiation within the embryonic cells occurs around day five after fertilization.

> *When the Word of God penetrates your heart, you become different.*

Spiritually speaking, the number five has been defined as the number of grace. It is by grace that we are saved and it is through salvation that transformation takes place in those that accept Christ as their savior. This transformation is what makes us "differentiate" and develop into the new creatures God has destined us to be. What an awesome parallel regarding when differentiation begins naturally and spiritually.

In the first trimester, it is difficult to know for sure whether normal differentiation of the embryonic cells is taking place. As a matter of fact, at times, abnormalities in proper development may not be identified until later in the pregnancy. With that said, there are first trimester screening test that have been designed to screen for the more common chromosomal abnormalities that can occur in pregnancy. The purpose of this screening test is to provide early detection of genetic abnormalities in case individuals desire to terminate the pregnancy or to simply know if their baby will be abnormal.

I think this is what is missing in spiritual pregnancies today: there is no one providing the appropriate screening to ensure that what is being carried is healthy and normal. *Why don't we?* Are we afraid of telling someone that what he or she is carrying is not consistent with the character or spiritual DNA of God? Are we afraid to be honest with people regarding their ability or need to terminate something that is not of God, for fear of disappointing them?

Honestly, what keeps us from addressing this important aspect of development within the Body of Christ? This is perhaps why we have so many spiritual births within the Kingdom of God that are not from God. As a result, many individuals exodus the church due to the confusion they experience when they see individuals moving in "giftings" that are not from God. For this reason, I believe it is imperative that the spiritual leaders within the churches of God throughout this world, begin to carefully examine the Body of Christ more attentively, and have the courage and boldness to inform individuals when the results obtained are contrary to the character and image of Christ. Even more challenging is the ability of leaders (upon finding abnormalities) to terminate what is not of God or intervene when necessary to ensure a Godly image is birthed.

I love first trimester visits because they are often filled with a great deal of excitement for many women and their families. At the same time, they are also filled with anxiety for many. The anxiety in the first trimester often centers around moms-to-be not knowing if what is growing inside of them is alive. You see, in the early part of the first trimester, although development is taking place, it cannot be seen or heard initially with the natural eyes or ears. This makes many women nervous, because although they've confirmed they are pregnant, the first thing every woman wants to know is whether what is developing inside of her is "alive." She wants to "hear" or "see" something that demonstrates viability. That means life.

Since, fetal heart tones cannot be heard until approximately 10-12 weeks of life (at the earliest), the ultrasound is often used to provide this reassurance for many. Every woman wants to know that what she is carrying inside of her is not dead. Likewise, you should want to know that what is developing inside of you is viable. Spiritual viability is just as important as the natural. Anything dead will not grow, neither naturally, nor spiritually.

Growth, however, can be normal or abnormal. Things of God develop and function normally. In the same way, things of the devil will also grow; however, because it is *not* of God, this growth will be abnormal and dysfunctional to God's design. Spiritually, how do you know if what is developing inside of you is viable? 2 Corinthians 13:5 gives us an answer. In it, you are instructed to "Examine yourselves to see whether you are in the faith; test yourselves. Do you not realize that Christ Jesus is in you--unless, of course, you fail the test?" (NIV). In order to know if what is developing inside of you spiritually is alive, you must examine yourself and make sure that what you find is in alignment with the scriptures.

The Bible tells us that Christ is life (John 14:6, NKJV). Therefore, when you begin to reflect the image of Christ (love, peace, forgiveness, etc.) through your life, you will know that what's inside of you is viable. What you are preparing to push out will be and should be the image of Christ. This image is simply made tangible to others through the method or manner He purposed for you to manifest it. For some this method may be a ministry, a book, an occupation, or another God-given purpose.

Finally, just like natural birth has an expected date of delivery (EDD, or due date), so does the spiritual realm. Natural pregnancy is based on 40 weeks. A woman is considered term (meaning mature) at 37 weeks and beyond. Normal delivery is anticipated anywhere between 37-40 weeks. God does not base each spiritual pregnancy on an identical set time frame. As it pertains to delivery, we must understand that His Word is clear that there is an appointed time and due season for one to birth forth what God is developing in him/her. Ecclesiastes 3:1 tells us "there is a time for everything, and a season for every activity under the heavens." (NKJV). Additionally, Jeremiah 29:11 reveals that like Jeremiah, God has an "expected end" (an appointed time) in mind for each and every one of us. (NKJV).

So, first trimester, is the time to determine viability, differentiate, screen for abnormalities, and develop. It is not a time for pushing, as it would be impossible to birth anything at this point. Moreover, pushing now would yield nothing because nothing has been positioned for delivery at this stage of the pregnancy. To push at this point would create nothing more than frustration, exhaustion, and potential injury—normal pregnancy will never produce anything at this stage.

The Second Trimester

"Hey, slow down," a passenger yells out to the large group of individuals pushing and shoving their way onto the metro train.

Imagine it is rush hour and everyone is tired and focused on their own goal and desire: to get to their final destination. The bell dings and the train doors close. Everyone is packed on the train like sardines. There is barely any room to move, and every seat has been taken by individuals looking pretty tired or just plain relaxed.

One of the passengers looks up to see a woman standing in the middle of the train, holding tightly onto the bar. Her back is tilted inwardly and her belly is protruding greatly over her feet. She is *clearly* pregnant. At once, the stranger seems to forget about himself and his feelings, and he quickly jumps up out of his seat and tells the woman to sit down. As others begin to notice the pregnant woman standing, she receives many offers to sit down immediately. Upon noticing the pregnant state of the woman, everyone became instantly concerned about her well-being and safety. No one wants her to fall and cause injury to herself or the precious gift she is carrying.

The second trimester consists of weeks 13-27 of a pregnancy. This trimester is all about *Growth and Development*. More specifically, it's all about an internal growth that now becomes visibly manifested. So it's very evident, not just to the pregnant person, but to others that there is a pregnancy developing. There *is* something growing inside of this individual. Remember, by the completion of the first 12 weeks of the pregnancy, everything—every cell necessary to develop every aspect of a human body is present: hair, bones, muscles, brain, lungs, heart, etc. Although present, they just have to undergo growth and development. In this second trimester, all primitive cells will begin to transform into their specified body part. Heart cells develop into the heart. Lung cells develop into the lungs. This medical fact, reminds me so much of the saying I use to hear in church quite often, which was "you are complete with Christ." This means that everything needed to succeed is already within you.

God has placed everything in you needed to be victorious in your life, to be what He has created you to be, and to fulfill His purpose. We are already completed because Christ is in us. What we are often going through in our lives as individuals, is *process*.

Push Vitamin

God has placed everything in you needed to be victorious in your life, to be what He has created you to be, and to fulfill His purpose

Process, is necessary so that what is already in us, and makes us complete, can now be developed and become visible. We are going through the transformation necessary for developing into the mature being that God has called us to be. Although I believe process is something we cannot control and, therefore, must simply "let go and let God;" I do believe that there are things we can do to progress. We will talk about that soon.

Growth is important because when things grow then we know that they are maturing. In every pregnancy, the anticipated endpoint is a mature fetus. We don't want premature deliveries, if possible, because premature deliveries have many risks that can compromise fetal well-being, health, life and viability. So, second trimester is mainly about "belly checks." Although there are a few other things done in this trimester (that we will discuss), this trimester of pregnancy focuses more on these "checks." These prenatal visits are usually straightforward and short in uncomplicated pregnancies. These "belly checks" involve measuring the patient's uterine size and verifying that it is consistent with how far along in pregnancy she is. Additionally, these visits continue to confirm that the newly developing creature is viable and developing properly.

As we walk with Christ over time, there should be a certain amount of growth seen that is consistent with how long we have been saved (in Christ). At times, I find some who have been saved for years but still act as babies in Christ and as if they don't know the Word. Apostle Paul in 1 Corinthians 3: 1-3, calls these individuals carnal—meaning immature. He further defines carnal as those that still demonstrate "envy, strife, and division" (NKJV). Sometimes in our humanness, we may fail to behave as a follower of Christ and exemplify His image. Other times, there are those who have chosen to completely walk away from God and no longer allow the growth they had experienced to be manifested outwardly through their behavior, communication, or thinking.

In His immense love for us, God understands our frailties, and forgives us at these moments. It is now up to us to realign ourselves with His Word so that we can continue to grow completely in Him. When we fail to accept His forgiveness, and continue to behave in ways contrary to God's Word, it can lead to our distraction away from the things of God. When this continues, we are at risk of following the plan of the devil for our lives and suffering a spiritual death of the purpose that is in us.

Many times, you do not know the Word of God, because you were not being developed. What makes us develop? In pregnancy, development is a divine process. We, as physicians, don't have anything to do with the growth process taking place inside the womb of a woman. The process is on automatic. The cells are growing, transforming, and developing the actual fetus. Although we monitor it, we cannot control it, nor change it.

Our bodies are divine in its development and the process that commonly takes place regarding growth, development, and its function. This is such a parallel to our spiritual growth, which too, is divine. Christ, who is the divine power of God, causes us to transform, become new creatures, and grow. If we will yield to the growth and what Christ is doing in us, then that growth will eventually produce maturity in all of us, as believers. This is what spiritual growth is about: that we are no longer "babes in Christ," but can get to a place where we can handle meat (1 Corinthians 3:2, KJV). This means we can handle the deeper things of the Word: the revelations, the mysteries, and the things illuminated by the Word.

Have you ever seen a woman five months pregnant, but you couldn't tell? You are surprised when she tells you this, because it is unnoticeable. Sometimes the inability of a woman to show at a time that one would commonly show could be due to her habitus, or body build. She may be a larger woman in which her body/fat composition may mask the ability for her to "show." Although other things can affect one's ability to show properly, including conditions that cause growth restriction, the point being made is that there is an expectation by most people (including physicians) that when you are pregnant, at some point you need to be showing and should be showing. This means that, objectively, people should be able to see your growth.

Growth should be visible. Just like the enlargement of a woman's uterus is obvious as she progresses further in her pregnancy, so should the enlargement of one's ability to demonstrate love, forgiveness, joy, righteousness, peace, temperance, goodness, meekness, faith, and so on. In other words, we should see the fruit of the spirit growing within us as we walk with God. As a physician, I want to be able to demonstrate that the uterine growth measures appropriately to the gestational age of the fetus. This growth should be increasing throughout the pregnancy and should be consistent with how far along one is in pregnancy. Same should be true with spiritual pregnancy.

In addition to the "belly checks," fetal heart tones are also monitored throughout the second trimester. The purpose of listening to the fetal heart tones is to confirm that what is developing inside of the uterus is viable and still alive. Anatomy scans are also routinely ordered in the second trimester between 18-20 weeks to examine the bodily structure of the baby. In the eyes of every patient, the anatomy scan is when she finds out the gender of the baby. Will it be a boy or a girl? However, this is an ultrasound that is looking at all of the structures of the baby: brain, legs, abdomen, heart, amniotic fluid levels, placenta location and size, and so on. Size measurements are obtained to be used as a reference point for growth. When the anatomy scan is normal, then it gives us a reassurance that the baby is developing normally. Additionally, it signifies that the process is operating as planned.

When the anatomy scan demonstrates an abnormality of some sort, now we begin to surveillance the pregnancy even closer because we get concerned about whether or not normal growth is at risk. Questions arise as to why this abnormality has arisen, or why the baby is measuring smaller, or larger. As a result of an abnormal ultrasound being obtained, repeat ultrasounds are now ordered to monitor the pregnancy closer, which is not needed during normal pregnancy.

Finally, we continue to answer questions that the patients may have regarding her pregnancy process, and evaluate her for the development of troublesome symptoms or signs. When found, intervention is often implemented.

Have you ever noticed the response a woman receives when people notice she is pregnant? It seems like at the moment they realize an individual is pregnant, their instinct to ensure the well-being of the pregnant woman increases. I've noticed that people seem to go out of their way to provide protection and safe-keeping of the unborn baby and mother-to-be. The presence of growth must be manifested outwardly and be noticeable. That's why the behavior of others towards the pregnant woman begins to change. It is visible change which, in and of itself, produces a response from others.

Think about it! It is the pregnant woman people will let go first in line. It is the pregnant woman people will give their seats to. It is the pregnant woman people will often rush to assist with certain tasks and activities. Even strangers are just as concerned with safeguarding the new creature developing within an expecting mom. Everyone wants to see to it that the expectant mom is rested and not tiring herself out. They are more sensitive to the extra "weight" mom is carrying and how she feels as a result. No one wants the mother to fall. This, as we know, could result in major harm or even the death (loss) of the baby. As a result, caring individuals are more vigilant of the mom-to-be and her environment.

The same type of care is necessary in the spiritually pregnant individual during this time. Similar to natural pregnancy, at some point in spiritual development, growth that has taken place internally should externally manifest and become visible to others. Likewise, when spiritual growth becomes evident within an individual within the Body of Christ, it ought to produce a response in others to want to "safeguard" the well-being of the "new creature."

Unfortunately, many in the kingdom of God, miss that essential principle. Instead, when individuals "get saved" and their spiritual growth begins, we, as leaders, often want to get them busy doing church work. Too often, the extensive busy "church work" leads to tiredness and eventually burn out because there is a lack of sensitivity regarding what the spiritually pregnant individual can handle. The need to "protect" the well-being of the developing new creature somehow becomes overshadowed by the feeling of the need to keep people busy. As a result, the opportunity for the spiritually pregnant individual to experience what most naturally pregnant women do is lost. Growth, although occurring, is often misunderstood, because a time of joy, discovery, and learning is lost.

Most pregnant women I see in my office, especially first time moms, are highly concerned with wanting to do everything right during their pregnancy. They are excited, curious, and aware that something wonderful is growing inside of them. They are often anxious about doing anything that will hurt the baby. As a result of their inquisition, these women are reading all sorts of books and other resources about pregnancy. Most commonly read is "What to Expect When You're Expecting." Expecting parents turn to this book to make sure they have an understanding of what to expect in each phase/trimester of pregnancy. They want to know:

- What signs and symptoms they are looking for?
- What's normal and abnormal?
- When do they need to address certain things with the doctor?
- What are the milestones of pregnancy?
- What will be done each pregnancy visit?
- How should they feel?
- What is going on inside of them?
- How big is the baby now?

It is not uncommon for my patients to come to their prenatal visits with a list of questions (to ask) written on a piece of paper.

When God's Word begins to produce new life and change within the believer, he or she needs a safe place to share what he or she is feeling or experiencing. The ability to ask questions without judgment is imperative. Many times we miss this fact, which is vital in the Kingdom of God. As leaders, we have to be more sensitive to those in our churches who are pregnant with the things of God, and as a result, are developing into new creatures. We must create consistent and specific time for the believer to ask the same questions: *What is going on inside of me? What are normal signs of spiritual development and what is abnormal? When do I need to address things with my spiritual leader. How should I feel throughout various stages of my spiritual walk?*

Instead of making believers so busy in the church, we need to be making sure they are rested. Rested—not just from a physical perspective, but also spiritually. Rested—meaning that they are not overburdened with work within the church. Rested—meaning that they are supported by fellow believers throughout their growing process. Rested—meaning that they are in the position to receive and embrace all that they are experiencing in this essential growing phase of their spiritual development. We, pastors and church leaders, need to be more sensitive to the load and the weight they're carrying and make sure that they are getting time to enjoy the spiritual process they are experiencing.

Similar to the natural pregnancy process, those who are spiritually expecting also need to be closely monitored throughout their process. Yes! Spiritual prenatal visits need to be in place. An example—regular appointments with a spiritual leader or mentor which will serve as the "safe place" for these individuals to ask questions and share what they are feeling about their growth process. Additionally, these visits will also serve to monitor their spiritual process to ensure that appropriate growth and development is taking place.

Is their growth consistent with where they are in their walk with Christ? They may not be reading "What to Expect When You're Expecting," however they need to be reading the Word of God and any other material that can help them understand "what to expect" throughout their spiritual walk. This can give them excitement about their spiritual growth. All believers need time to understand what God is doing in him or her. As a result, authentic and mature leaders need to be present to specifically explain what may be going on within them throughout various phases of their walk with Christ.

Spiritual leaders, like obstetricians, are the ones responsible for managing and delivering what is to be birthed. Often times, leaders are not as sensitive to the spiritually pregnant individuals around them. We often assume that everyone is pregnant at the same time, and all have the same due date. Not so! If the natural does not work this way, then neither will the spiritual. Women in the first and second trimester of pregnancy are not ready nor supposed to be ready to push! Likewise, just because someone is in the third trimester, still doesn't mean they are ready to push!

There is an appointed time to push. Any pushing prior to that appointed time will not result in delivery. Only frustration and potentially injury will develop when one pushes outside of the specified time. Leaders, everyone will not deliver at that same time. It is important to gauge who's ready to push so that the whole Body (meaning the church) is not trying to push and deliver at the same time. Remember, some may be premature and some may be ready to push; some may even be past due. My fellow church colleagues please "Know those that labor among you!"

The second trimester is all about growth. Growth meaning "increase." When things begin to increase in size, diameter, and number—that is growth. When I think of growth, I also think of height. Yes, height! Why? Because height is defined as "extent upward" (Apple online dictionary). Extent meaning "proportion, size, expanse, or dimensions" (Apple online dictionary).

In pediatrics, the increase in a child's height is often a measurement used to determine if he or she is growing adequately. It's something that is visually appreciated. I believe that in the same way there is an increase in growth naturally, spiritually—growth should involve increase.

If you say you've been saved for a while and living by the Word of God, and you say that you are abiding in Christ and He is abiding in you, then as a new creature one ought to see increase at some point. Increase, meaning you are not remaining stagnant, however, you are ascending to higher dimensions in the Lord. Moreover, when it's all said and done, your spiritual increase should be visually appreciated by those around you. Just like a developing child whose increasing height depicts adequate growth, so it should be in the child of God. When we don't see increase in the life of the believer, we need to ask, why that is? What is stifling the process, and therefore, the growth?

Since the second trimester is all about growth, this is not the trimester that you would be pushing. In fact, it is medically impossible in normal pregnancy to push at this stage. It is not the time to push, but in fact that time to grow, develop, and manifest outwardly what is occurring on the inside. It is a time to be more aware of what is going on in your body.

During this trimester, women begin to feel flutters of fetal movement and eventually distinct baby kicks. From this experience, they begin to understand what the new creature developing inside them feels like. Most women begin to get a better understanding of the behavior pattern of their baby. This provides knowledge regarding vital information: when the baby moves more, morning or evening; what they feel in their body throughout the baby's development; how they personally feel during this stage, and which foods they believe the baby likes or doesn't like.

It's the same way spiritually. As we are becoming that new creature in Christ and Christ is developing new things in us, we ought to get to a place where we start to feel and become more sensitive to the movement of the Holy Spirit in us. Sensitive to when Christ is nudging and moving us to do something. For some of us, we may need to be aware of when Christ is "kicking us" to get our attention, or to move in a certain area. It is imperative that we become more aware of the pattern in which Christ may deal with us individually.

How does the Lord deal with you? Does He speak to you softly in a "still small voice?" Does He use other people to get your attention? You must develop an awareness of what Christ is doing in you. You need to develop for yourself an understanding that what Christ is doing in your life is alive. Until you get to that place, you will need to stay close to those who can listen to what is inside of you and confirm that it is still viable and alive in God. In time, you yourself will begin to know that what God is doing on the inside of you is real.

Often times, it is such a surreal experience for women to be pregnant. They know they are pregnant initially because we, as physicians, are telling them they are, or because we have shown them an ultrasound that verifies they are pregnant. They know, not because they themselves can feel it or see it, but only because someone else they trust has spoken it. However, many times it doesn't usually become "real" to a woman until she herself has been able to feel the first movement, kick, or flutter. Then, there is this reassurance that she is carrying something which is alive! She is carrying a blessing and something *(or should I say someone)* who will be the image of her and the father of this baby.

We ought to feel that same way spiritually. When we begin to feel the movement of God within us, we should develop an excitement that *I am carrying and in the process of birthing something Christ has placed in me.* Furthermore, there should be a realization that *I am not only carrying something that Christ is developing in me, however—it is alive!* As a result, it is a blessing and it will bring life to others. More importantly, one should finally realize that in addition to what God has placed in us that is growing, Christ Himself is also residing in us and giving rise to our personal and spiritual growth and development.

Many pregnant women, upon coming to the realization that what is developing inside of them is real, will become more careful regarding how they handle their pregnancy. Those who smoke will usually stop or cut down significantly. Those who consume a moderate amount of junk food, will become more health conscious regarding what they eat. These changes are often prompted after the mom-to-be has felt movement, seen, or heard the fetal heartbeat. This experience gives her the desire to quickly change any behavior that could negatively impact the health of the baby. She doesn't want to do anything that could harm the baby or cause her to lose the pregnancy.

Most parents-to-be will manage and protect what is developing inside of the mother. It's instinctual for most. As a result, many will also accept their responsibility to obey the doctor's instructions regarding what is necessary for them to do to ensure that the baby will have a healthy outcome. Spiritually we have got to have the same mindset. We have got to guard and protect, by our behavior, the purpose, greatness and gifts that God is developing inside of us. As a result, we must be careful regarding who we connect and communicate with. We must also pay heed to the behaviors we take part in. It is important we ensure that we are doing everything possible to obey the instructions given spiritually and naturally to avoid compromising what is developing inside of us.

Finally, the second trimester is usually when food cravings begin. These cravings can become so strong that they often cause women to seek out what they desire, no matter the time or day. The same thing should be occurring at this stage of development in spiritual pregnancy. The new believers should begin to develop a strong spiritual food craving. Peter 2:2 says, "Like newborn babies, crave pure spiritual milk, so that by it you may grow up in your salvation" (NKJV). The Word of God is the spiritual milk.

New believers ought to have a hunger and thirst for the Word of God. They ought to crave it so badly that they will make the sacrifices to "taste and see that the Lord is good" (Psalm 34:8). We know that the Lord is Jesus Christ and we know that Jesus Christ *is* the Word made flesh. Therefore, we should see a craving for more of the Word of God from the new believer as they grow more in their spiritual walk.

The Third Trimester

The third trimester consists of weeks 28-40 of pregnancy. Most define its end with delivery of the fetus. Throughout the third trimester, the woman's belly is becoming larger and rapid growth of the fetus is taking place as she nears the expected date of delivery. Uterine measurements and fetal heart tones continue to be monitored and assessed. Although the focus still remains on growth, the third trimester is all about *Maturity*. Maturation of the developing fetus and preparation for delivery is important during this trimester.

This trimester, although exciting because one is closer to delivery, also seems to be frustrating for many. This is the trimester in which my patients are often waddling into the exam room, and all seem to express the same theme of conversation, "I'm tired of being pregnant." The complaints during these office visits usually include abdominal pressure, back pain, swelling, and just plain old discomfort. Additionally, patients often complain of their inability to sleep well at night because they often can't get comfortable enough to rest.

I've noticed this same type of feeling arising in many believers as they near the appointed time that God is planning to expose (deliver) to others, the gifts or calling He has placed in them. After a time of preparation and growth, many become restless with God and "tired" of waiting for Him to expose to others what He has placed inside of them. Whether it's ministry, gifts, or a particular calling within the Body of Christ, this is a time when the believer wants so desperately for God to "hurry up" and use them so that what is in them can be revealed to others.

Like the tiring mother in the last stage of pregnancy who "just wants the baby out," so it is with the believer who becomes impatient with God's process of development and maturity and also "wants it out." They begin to feel more pressure (often from themselves) to bring forth the ministry, the purpose, or the dream they feel God has placed inside of them. This is a critical time, because it is where more complaints and murmuring arise due to the discomfort encountered. It is a time where many of my obstetrical patients will often beg for me to "take the baby out."

The problem with this is that many times it is too early to deliver. Furthermore, an early delivery could cause severe compromise to the fetus. Unfortunately, discomfort is a natural part of the process and must be endured until the appointed time of delivery. Ironically, the same must be realized in spiritual pregnancy. To deliver prematurely always has a risk of injury. Patience must be implemented when waiting for God to birth forth from us, what He has placed inside. The journey to maturity is not always easy or comfortable, but it is necessary.

So let's talk about maturity! "Maturation is the process of achieving full development and growth" (Behrman & Butler, *Preterm Birth Causes, Consequences, and Prevention*, 2007). It is a term used throughout the field of medicine to describe maximal development of various organs, tissue, or systems of the human body. In May 1972, an article was written in the American Journal of Obstetrics & Gynecology by Dewhurst et al, regarding "The Assessment of Fetal Maturity and Dysmaturity." In this article the authors sought to define what a mature fetus was. Their initial definition of a mature fetus was "one which had gained the maximum benefit from its intrauterine existence" (1972). However, they later revealed that this definition contained a major flaw. The flaw was that two factors, versus one, were needed in order for a fetus to be considered mature. Below I've included the actual segment of the article illuminating their findings.

"In attempting a definition of maturity we evolved the notion that a mature fetus was one which had gained the maximum benefit from its intrauterine existence. This seemed satisfactory at first but later we became aware of its fallacies.

The fetus may obtain the maximum benefit from its intrauterine existence while it is still clearly immature; to use an obvious example a fetus which dies in utero on any particular day during pregnancy had plainly gained the maximum benefit from its intrauterine existence at some earlier time; but since it may by that time have reached only one or 2 pounds in weight it cannot be considered mature.

It then became evident that two factors are concerned, not one; a mature fetus we decided was one which had gained the maximum benefit from an intrauterine existence of approximately 40 weeks duration. The two factors concerned are: (1) time in utero, for growth and development to occur, and (2) placental support to make growth possible. Neither factor alone is sufficient—there may be excellent placental support for growth but if the child is expelled too soon for any reason whatsoever it may die of immaturity; alternatively with poor placental support the child may die in utero long before term is reached."

Wow! What revelation! Growth needs time in a particular place and someone or something to make it possible. From the article we learn that *time* in a surrounding or environment alone, is not enough for a fetus to become mature. However, placental support is just as essential. If you have one without the other, the author is clear, maturity cannot and will not take place.

If the human fetus, developing in the protected surrounding of the womb cannot become mature simply by the time spent inside of the womb, then why do we in the Body of Christ think we can become mature simply by the *time* spent in the protected surroundings of our churches? It's evident many feel this way in the Body of Christ or otherwise we would not have a tremendous amount of individuals being considered mature and promoted to leadership positions, simply based on how long they have been serving in the church.

I've seen it many times throughout my life, and I've also seen many of these same leaders fall due to their immaturity as a result of never having the proper *support* during their tenure in the Body of Christ. Yes! They were serving all those years! Yes! They were faithful in church all those years! Unfortunately, maturity still did not take place because of the lack of support by others in the Kingdom. By support, I mean someone they were solely connected to for a specified period of time, and who provided nourishment and life. We will come back to this principle in a few. In the meantime, I want to focus on the two factors that the authors revealed are needed for a developing fetus to become mature.

Although the Dewhurst, et al. (1972) piece is a medical article, it is filled with so much revelation and spiritual parallels, especially as it pertains to what is needed for maturity to be obtained. I want to focus on the two factors given for what defines "mature fetus." The two factors given in this article are:

1. Time in utero; and

2. Placental support to make growth possible.

Time in utero is self-explanatory. However, placental support may need some expounding.

So, what is a placenta! You may be wondering. The placenta is a flat, circular reddish-purple organ attached to the inside of the uterus. Its reddish purple color is largely due to its vast composition of blood vessels. Functionally, this phenomenal organ supports and maintains the pregnancy by supplying the fetus with nutrients and oxygen from the mother. With a complex blood vessel system, the placenta acts as a connector between mom and baby made possible by the umbilical cord. The role and function of the placenta is absolutely essential to the viability of any pregnancy. No pregnancy can survive in the absence of placental support.

As mentioned previously, placental support involves the provision of nutrients and oxygen from the mom to the developing fetus. Remember, within the womb, the fetus is unable to eat and drink normal food to obtain sustenance. As a result, the placenta transfers these necessary nutrients to baby (from mom) through the elaborate blood vessel system via the umbilical cord. Additionally, the placenta also acts as a filter in an attempt to keep harmful things from getting to the baby (i.e. – infections). *Sometimes you need someone connected to you that will help you filter out what's good and bad until you are mature enough to do it for yourself. Moreover, you need this person to not only cover you; but to provide a safe haven (like the womb) while you are yet figuring it out.*

In the Body of Christ, I rarely find a church that has developed a complex system whereby individuals are connected to someone who can provide nourishment and care for their spiritual survival. Please understand, that I'm not talking about the pastors who deliver a great word from their pulpit, feed the congregation, and provide spiritual nutrients to their flock. No! I'm talking about a structure developed outside of the pastor's pulpit. I'm talking about a support system beyond the pastor himself. I'm talking about something structured and long term.

Maturity requires time and support.

Many pastors assume that because they are delivering a great Word, that they are feeding their flock adequately. They further assume that if people are not growing it's because "they are not eating the good Word that is being delivered to them." Although this could be very true, the problem with this thought process is when it stops here. Remember, the placenta has to supply the fetus with nutrients in utero because the fetus is unable to feed itself. It **can't** eat. It does not have the capacity to accept actual solid food. It can only receive nutrients that have been broken down from the food ingested by the mother.

Likewise, even after birth, the ability for a child to eat certain food consistencies and feed him/herself develops over time. You can put a piece of cake in front of a newborn, and he won't touch it or eat it because he can't! The same holds true in the Body of Christ regarding the preached word; this is why other support systems are necessary to the development of maturity in the believer.

So what should this support system look like in the Body of Christ? I think it should look much like the in utero system God designed. In this system the mom and baby are connected by the placenta via the umbilical cord. The umbilical cord is the "life line" connecting both. Normally the umbilical cord is a three vessel cord, meaning it consists of two arteries and one vein. Ecclesiastes 4:12 teaches us that, "Though one may be overpowered, two can defend themselves. A cord of three strands is not quickly broken" (NIV). This scripture clearly demonstrates that although one person may be "overpowered" by his enemy when fighting alone; two people coming together, representing 2 strands, are able to defend. Their ability to defend is due to the fact that Christ Himself joins the two and becomes the third strand.

I believe that churches need to develop support systems whereby believers are paired together as a team. Like the *buddy system* we were forced to implement in elementary school while growing up. Like our elementary school buddy system, the purpose of this support system is to provide protection, accountability, safety, and fellowship. Spiritually speaking, this connection should always consist of a mature believer being connected to either a new babe in Christ or maybe one that is still in the process of reaching maturity. Furthermore, Christ

Himself must be the connector.

Similar to obstetrics, this connection must be for a longer vs. shorter period of time to assure maturity being reached. Remember, the author in the article revealed that "a mature fetus was one who gained the maximum benefit from an intrauterine existence of approximately 40 weeks duration." In other words, there is a certain amount of time needed to assure maturity is reached. Even today in obstetrics, 40 weeks is considered the duration of the normal pregnancy process. By 40 weeks maturity is assured although it can occur as early as 37 weeks, which is why pregnancy is considered "term" at that point.

Prematurity, involves the expelling/delivery of the fetus prior to 37 weeks, causing the placental connection between mom and baby to be separated too early. When the placenta separates earlier than it should from the uterine wall (placental abruption), fetal death is a great risk. This is due to the disruption of oxygen and nutrients to the growing baby. Likewise, if the placenta does not function properly in any way, the growth and life of the baby is also at risk.

Spiritually, it is the same. When we disconnect from the babes in Christ earlier than the appointed time (spiritual abruption), many of them experience spiritual death in one way or another. Some-

> *When we disconnect from the babes in Christ earlier than the appointed time (spiritual abruption), many of them experience spiritual death in one way or another.*

times it may be in a specific area, and sometimes it can be in general. Other times, the abruption may not cause death, but lead to a premature delivery of the gift that was developing inside of the believer. This is why it is important that the "buddy" support systems, if implemented within the church, must be for a longer, versus shorter, period of time. The 6-week new member's class, the 1-day leadership workshop, the periodic pastoral appointments, are just not enough to produce maturity. Longer periods of time involving more intimate support is what is needed.

Now, we must be careful that the support systems implemented are healthy connections that do not hinder the delivery of what is developing inside of the believer. I say this because in obstetrics, when the placenta attaches abnormally, it hinders normal delivery. An example of this is *placenta previa*. Placenta previa is an abnormal attachment in which the placenta attaches over top of the opening to the birth canal. Whether partially or completely covering the entryway to the birth canal, it still prevents normal delivery by obstructing the baby's ability to move out of the womb. As a result, a C-section is warranted when delivery is needed or eminent. Vaginal bleeding is a life threatening complication of placenta previa and can cause a serious obstetrical emergency.

People to whom we are connected can sometimes do the same: become so attached to someone and so invested in the desire to support them that they themselves may obstruct the delivery of what God wants to birth through the individual they are helping. This obstruction can be due to things they say or do that negatively affect the very one they have been connected with to help.

Another example of an abnormal placental attachment is *placenta accreta*. This condition involves the invasion of the placental tissue extensively into the uterine wall. The resulting complication is the inability of the placenta to easily separate from the uterine wall after delivery of the fetus. As a result, life-threatening bleeding often occurs. In severe cases, an emergent hysterectomy is performed due to hemorrhaging which can lead to death. The result of the hysterectomy is the inability to bear more children.

Sadly, this *placenta accreta* occurs in the Body of Christ on a spiritual level. I've seen people become so deeply and extensively connected to others that they often cause them to lose their ability to spiritually produce. These individuals I call "fertility killers." These individuals at times are struggling with jealousy and envy. Other times it can be overbearingness, worry, or micromanagement. Nevertheless, the connection is not fruitful over time.

The final example is the *retained placenta*. This placenta remains inside the uterus after the specified time given after delivery of the baby (30 minutes). A retained placenta is not always a placenta accreta; however, a placenta accreta will always be retained. The complications of a retained placenta can be vaginal bleeding or maternal infection. Its removal often requires surgical intervention. The spiritual parallelism lies within the fact that some individuals desire to remain connected to others even after God's appointed time for the connection has ended.

Many times God will assign an individual to another for a specific purpose or a specific season (time). When that purpose has been fulfilled, there are times that God will remove that individual from that specific role. The problem, however, is that many (for selfish reasons) remain in the same role despite God's instruction. As a result, the relationship is negatively impacted and in many instances begins to deteriorate.

So we've already discussed the nutrient supply function of the placenta; however, the placenta also has another critical function. This function involves the placenta's amazing responsibility to support the pregnancy by providing oxygen to the fetus. Many of my patients do not realize, until birth, that the fetus does not take its first breath until after delivery. Until the time of delivery, it is the placenta which acts as a lung by carrying oxygen from the maternal circulation to the fetus through the umbilical cord. In order to fully understand, its intricacy, I will review briefly the physiology of how the lung works once we are born.

When we take our first breath, as humans, we breathe in air which contains oxygen. The breathed in air received by our lungs diffuses the oxygen from the air into our bloodstream. The oxygen then attaches to red blood cells traveling within the blood vessels of the lungs. Once the oxygen is in the bloodstream, it is pumped throughout our entire body by our cardiac system to supply the needed oxygen to every organ and tissue within the body. Now, when we exhale, our body is releasing a waste product called carbon dioxide. If it is not released, it can build up and cause death.

Okay, so back to the placenta as the oxygen supplier to the fetus. Since the baby cannot breathe yet, the placenta transports oxygen from the mother to the baby via the umbilical cord vein. Once the oxygen rich blood has circulated throughout the fetus' entire body and been consumed, waste products are then carried back to the mother's circulation through the umbilical cord arteries. Once the waste products have entered into mom's circulation, she will excrete it from her body through urination. This is such a powerful revelation that human nature is revealing to us. The spiritual revelation is "that sometimes we need someone to filter, carry, and dump our waste, so that we can live."

So up to this point, we have discussed what is needed for one to be considered mature (time and support). So when these two essential things occur in normal pregnancy, maturity always takes place. So what does fetal maturity look like in the third trimester?

According to the American Pregnancy Association and the Mayo Clinic online there are many things that develop in the fetus, during the third trimester, that are characteristic of maturity. Development of fetal maturity becomes evident when the baby's bones become fully developed—the baby's eyes open completely and the baby is able to detect light, fetal growth occurs rapidly, the baby develops a firm grasp, and baby positions itself for delivery into a vertex position (head down).

Spiritually, we should begin to see these same types of things develop in the believer who is nearing maturity or has become mature. Just like the fetus has the ability to open its eyes wide and detect light, so the mature believer should be able to do the same. Jesus said, "I am the way, the truth, and the light…" Thus when one is mature, he or she should be able to detect the Light (Christ). By detect, I mean that the mature believer should be able to discern Christ's Spirit, recognize Christ's voice, and be able to identify the presence of Christ in his or her life. Rapid growth in the believer then should take place as he nears delivery of what God has placed in Him.

Additionally, just like the grasp of the fetus becomes firm in the third trimester, allowing the baby to now begin to hold on to things, so should the grasp (comprehension) of the mature believer, regarding the Word of God, be firm in order that he or she is able to "holdfast to the teachings" of the Lord and "stand firm in the faith," as 2 Thessalonians 2:15 and 1 Corinthians 16:13 commands.

Now, let's talk about the bone development in the mature fetus. Completion of the development of the fetal bones in the third trimester is important because this means that the framework for the body has been completed. Bones are unique organs that make up the human skeleton. Bones consist of three parts: collagen, calcium-phosphate, and living bone cells. The function of bones is not only to give shape and form to the body, but it also supports, protects vital organs, and provides mobility to the entire body. Finally, as a living organ, some bones (long) contain marrow which produce the necessary blood cells to sustain life. Bones, as the skeletal framework, are the foundation of the body itself. Remember, bones keep us upright and moving. Without bones, we would be nothing more than a big blob of immobile formless tissue.

Isn't it interesting that the earth itself was "without form and void and darkness was upon the land" (Gen 1:2) until God intervened? Once the Trinity intervened, God the Father, the Son & the Holy Spirit brought form into the earth. This is what happens in our lives when Christ enters. The darkness of sin is removed and we now become the form of Godliness. The believer is able to become the form of Godliness simply because Christ, along with the Godhead, like human bones has now become the "framework" for the believer.

As the spiritual framework, the Godhead not only shapes the believer into the "image of Christ," but by the presence of Christ and through the power of the Holy Spirit, it provides support, protection, mobility, and life. Abundant life is produced and sustained through Jesus Christ Himself, who functions as the marrow of the Trinity, producing life-giving blood to the new creature (Proverbs 3:7-8). This blood purifies and cleanses (1 John 1:7, Rev. 1:5). As one matures in the faith, he gives full control to Christ to direct his life. As a result, this spiritual framework—like bones—keeps the believer "upright and moving by the Spirit of God." Moreover, it allows the new creature to "live, move, and have its being in Him" (Acts 17:28, NKJV). It provides a solid foundation within the believer, for everything else to grow.

Grow, grow, grow. All throughout the pregnancy, that's what

the fetus has been doing, growing and increasing in size. In the beginning of pregnancy, there was a great deal of room within the uterus for the maturing fetus to move. However, in the third trimester, the room for movement becomes limited due to the increase in baby's size and the decrease in the intrauterine space. The uterus is nearing it's maximum stretch capacity which causes the baby to be more confined. As a result, most babies instinctively (or inherently) position themselves head down towards the birth canal in preparation and readiness of its *estimated date of delivery*. In obstetrics we say, "the baby is vertex." Vertex meaning the head is down and is the presenting part for delivery (vs. the feet).

When the head is down, normal delivery is anticipated. However, when the feet (or any other part of the baby) presents first, normal delivery cannot take place, necessitating a C-section to be performed at time of delivery. What revelation! That a fetus, would instinctively know to change its posture so that its delivery could take place and allows it to finally be manifested to an awaiting group of people. It's as if the baby is demonstrating an understanding of its need to submit to a divine plan.

God's plan is always to deliver to an awaiting group of people what He is maturing inside of the believer. Like the body of the growing fetus that begins to fill up the space inside of the uterus necessitating delivery at some appointed time, so too will the believer be "brought to fullness" in Christ and become in need of delivery (Col. 2:10). The problem, however, for many of us, is that we fail to position ourselves in the correct posture for delivery. "Head down!" This position can represent submission, along with other things.

Unfortunately, many believers struggle with submitting to the plan of God for their lives by resisting the process of growth and development that God is often taking them through. As these believers near their divine *estimated date of delivery* and commencement of labor, plans for delivery must be adjusted as normal birth cannot take place and pushing will not occur.

> **MEN'S PERSPECTIVE**
>
>
>
> *Pregnancy Growth & Development*
>
> **Me:** *What were your thoughts when you begin to witness my body manifesting the obvious changes of pregnancy?*
>
> **Greg:** *Absolutely beautiful!*

I knew Greg's response to this question was true because it is exactly what he communicated to me throughout my pregnancy as my belly began to increase in size. He was enthralled with my abdomen, and everything else that was expanding. He was fascinated with the entire process and demonstrated it consistently throughout my process.

Pregnancy was something Greg truly celebrated from visualizing life growing inside of me with the kicks and movements of the baby, to seeing life as a pregnant mother change me. Even if I didn't feel beautiful, I believed I was beautiful because he told me enough times that I was.

Likewise, it is also important to have individuals in your life who will celebrate what God is doing in you. The development of new life is always beautiful. Anytime someone has a chance to experience new life: whether through salvation or a new start after a tragic event, it must be celebrated. It is necessary that we have authentic individuals in our life who will celebrate the milestones we reach and the changes we make. It's what keeps people going and it's what builds faith within them.

Believe it or not, words are powerful and have the ability to give life or kill the spirit of a person. Just today, I witnessed a mom telling her son that he was "sorry." Not sorry, as in apologizing, but sorry as in "you're a loser." Wow! I could not believe I was witnessing such conversation; however, I am aware that this type of homicidal language is perpetuated every day in homes, on jobs, and even in churches.

Proverbs 18:21 says, "the tongue has the power of life and death" (NIV). Similar to Greg, are you using your words to affirm and celebrate the beauty of what you see developing in others? When we enter into new life with Christ, the transformation that takes place in our lives emits absolute beauty! The beauty is due to the image of Christ that we begin to manifest within us. It draws people. It captivates and fascinates many.

Finally, be mindful of the company you keep. If you fellowship with those who do not celebrate you, but instead discourage you or abuse you, then you yourself are at risk of becoming hardened and like them. 1 Corinthians 15:33 says, "Do not be deceived: Bad company corrupts good morals" (NLV). Keeping good company directly affects the health and well-being of what you birth.

SEVEN

The Labor Process

The tall, coffee-toned woman is standing in the bathroom shower. It is morning time and she is preparing to start her day. It is me. The night was not restful, as I experienced mild cramping throughout. The hot water beat down on my slender back as I began to wash my body. Suddenly, my belly began to tighten. The intense pain gripped me so tightly that it inhibited my ability to stand upright, forcing me to bend over in agony. I tried to grab the shower wall but was unable to take hold. As the pain eased, I began to yell for help. Within seconds, another agonizing tightening of my belly commenced. I tried to get out of the shower, but the intensity of the pain paralyzed me. I remained trapped within the confines of the shower tub. Like a soldier, I held my stance enduring each wave of suffering. *These are contractions. Labor has finally started*, I thought.

The painful contractions continued for 30 minutes and then as abruptly as they began, they ceased. Standing upright, I exited the shower. Once again, I began to call out for assistance, unsure if the pain would return again. My mother, Ivory, had already arrived. Grabbing my hand, she guided me out of the shower tub and gently wrapped a towel around me. Together we walked to my bedroom.

"Call the hospital," my mom instructed.

I picked up the phone and began to dial the number to the hospital. It was ringing. I waited anxiously for someone on the other end to answer. Promptly, the ringing stopped.

"Sparrow Hospital OB triage. How may I help you?"

I replied, "My name is Chevelta Smith, I'm 39 weeks pregnant and I've been having some contractions this morning."

"Ms. Smith, who's your doctor?"

"Dr. Diotti."

"Okay Great! Can you tell me how often you are contracting?"

"I was contracting every 1-2 minutes."

"How long have you been contracting?"

"I had contractions for a half hour and then they stopped. Occasionally, I feel some cramping."

"Okay Great! Normally, we want you to come in after you've been contracting every 2-5 minutes apart for a whole hour. Your contractions do not sound regular yet, and you still sound comfortable. Why don't you wait a little longer to see if the contractions get closer together?"

"Okay!"

I hung up the phone. My mother peered intently at me in anticipation of knowing what instructions I had received from the hospital clinician. I began to tell her the details of the discussion. She listened attentively, yet I could tell, she was not happy with the plan. I excused myself to go to the restroom. *This baby always seemed to be sitting on my bladder!*

Propping myself on the "white throne," I began to tinkle. I continued to feel mild cramping but nothing as severe as what I experienced earlier. *I wondered why the contractions had stopped.* As usual, I looked at the toilet paper after wiping. It was different this time. There was blood present. Although it was small, *a tiny speck, to be exact,* it was still blood and it was bright red.

"Mom! Come here!

She entered the bathroom quickly to find me holding up the soiled piece of toilet paper, like a little girl showing off an original piece of artwork.

"Look! There's blood!"

Bending over, she stared sharply at the little piece of paper, as though investigating a clue. She quickly stood upright and commanded, "Call the hospital! This time tell them you saw blood. When you say blood, they are definitely going to tell you to come in. "Trust me!" *Medically, blood always warrants a response. Spiritually, it is no different. Thank God for The Blood.*

In obedience, I called the hospital telling them everything she said, just like she said to say it! I hung up the phone and looked at my mother, who was once again staring intently at my face.

"What did they say?" she inquired.

"They said come on in to the Labor and Delivery floor to be evaluated."

"I knew it. Let's go," she said.

I arrived at Sparrow Hospital shortly thereafter, and was taken up to the Women and Children's wing by wheelchair. As my husband pushed me down the hall, I greeted everyone I saw in the hospital with a smile and a wave. This was so much different than how I arrived to the hospital with my first child! Then, the *painful contractions caused me to fall out of the wheelchair and onto my knees. I remember feeling the uncontrollable urge to push and the women commanding me not to push, despite my continuous cry "I gotta puuuuuuushhhh!"* The memories where still quite fresh!

My second birth was much less chaotic. This time I was taken to a triage room and given a hospital gown. The nurse came in to meet me and get all my information. Within moments, a resident doctor appeared to examine me. She seemed irritated that I was there. She checked my cervix and then looking at me sharply, she firmly stated, "you are only 2-3 centimeters dilated. I don't think you are in labor. Your contractions are not even regular, they are registering every 8-15 minutes and you don't seem to really be feeling them."

As she stepped back from in between my legs, the doctor on call immediately walked in and asked to repeat the exam. He was the attending physician. I consented. As the resident stepped to the side of the bed, he put on sterile gloves and gently began to recheck my cervix. It was uncomfortable, however I understood the need.

"Chevelta, you are 6 centimeters," he said as he stood up from completing the exam.

I quickly looked at the resident doctor, who had just checked me. How did she get it wrong? That was a huge difference. I then realized she is in training. It wasn't intentional, simply due to her lack of experience.

"I have to apologize, you are in TRUE labor, which means that your cervix is making change with the contractions you are having, although they are irregular," the attending physician further stated.

"The way you were looking, and the irregular pattern of your contractions, I just didn't think you were in labor. We are going to get you admitted. You are going to have a baby!"

Early on in my OB/Gyn residency, I learned the difference between "true labor" and "false labor." It was imperative that I learned it quickly in my career in order that I would know how to properly triage the many women I would evaluate over my lifetime.

True labor, by definition, often involves regular contractions that are painful and persistent despite positioning, and cause the cervix to open or dilate. False labor is often defined as irregular contractions that are often weak, may disappear with repositioning of the body, and does not cause the cervix to open. Remember, this is why the doctor on call did not think I was in labor, because I was not experiencing regular painful contractions. I have learned both medically and spiritually, that sometimes your course to delivery may not be the same as others. Moreover, at times God may cause you to progress in a way that is not typical. Nevertheless, we must learn to trust God to reveal when we are truly in the process of nearing delivery.

The only thing that verified I was in true labor was the fact that my cervix was dilated significantly. You see, although pregnancy is all about PROCESS, labor, however is all about PROGRESS! In other words, it's all about forward movement and advancement! More specifically: Change. Cervical change, that is! As obstetricians, our focus in determining and managing the labor process is based on whether or not the cervix made change.

Cervical change? Some of you may be wondering, "What is a cervix?" Well, let's briefly review the female anatomy as it pertains to obstetrics. I'll start with an illustration that hopefully will help. The womb actually has the shape of a balloon. Visualize for a moment a balloon that you have just blown up. Now let's pretend for a moment that a balloon could be blown up and stay blown up without putting a knot in the neck part of it. Okay. Can you see that in your mind?

Now then, let's use this balloon to demonstrate the various parts of the womb. Let's start from the bottom, which is where the opening to the balloon exists. This is the circular part you put to your mouth to start blowing air inside. This would represent the external cervix. Now, if you notice, there is a hole in the middle of this circular part which allows the air to pass inside. This leads into the slender portion of the balloon. *I call it "the neck."* However, this is where the knot is placed after the balloon is blown up. For medical comparison, this would be considered the neck of the cervix—specifically, the endocervical canal. This canal extends the length of the cervix and serves as the throughway between the uterus and the vagina.

Finally, we have the very end of the balloon. This is the largest segment of the balloon where all the air collects. It is the part of the balloon that expands as more air is blown inside of it. If you were looking at a real womb, this would be the area where the growing baby resides throughout pregnancy. The opening at the very top of the canal that leads into this part is called the inner cervix (internal os). This is the portion of the cervix that must dilate completely for pushing to begin. Okay now! Let's get back to cervical change.

During the labor process, many things are changing! The quiescent state of the uterus has changed. It is no longer at rest, but is active. It is contracting. Contractions are painful, on-and-off tightening of the uterine muscles. In true labor, these contractions cause the cervix to dilate (open) and squeeze the baby down further into the birth canal, causing the position of the baby's head to change. The environment surrounding the baby changes.

The baby has lived in a fluid filled sac throughout the entire pregnancy. However, during labor, that changes! It changes because at some point during labor the amniotic fluid sac will rupture spontaneously or will be artificially broken. The position of the fetus also changes.

There are actually seven distinct positional changes that the fetus will exhibit during the labor process. They are Engagement, Descent, Flexion, Internal Rotation, Extension, External Rotation, and

Expulsion. In obstetrics, we call them the Seven Cardinal movements of Labor. Although important, a detailed discussion of each is far beyond the scope of this book and would be more overwhelming if anything. We will briefly discuss these movements later in the chapter.

At this point, what I do want to focus on regarding these movements is the following principles of change that must occur in the presenting part (the head) of the baby in order for it to fit through the birth canal. When these seven changes do not occur appropriately, it can prevent spontaneous delivery of the fetus. Contractions, although usually painful, create a pressure which squeezes the baby down through the birth canal. It is this pressure that moves baby further down the birth canal (descent) thus allowing the head of the baby to be molded or "shaped " to fit through the birth canal. This shaping takes place as a result of the positional changes the fetal head must undergo in order to be delivered.

This same principle is important spiritually. Change must occur in your head, meaning your mind. I've often noticed that when God is preparing the believer to birth forth what is inside, an external pressure usually arises in the life of the believer. It is this pressure that begins to push the believer towards the door of opportunity that God has created and intended for him or her. However, in order to fit through this door, God will often allow this pressure to not only move the believer down the divine path He's planned (descent), but also cause the gift inside to conform to the necessary path in order that it can be delivered to those awaiting. If your mind is not conformed or molded to fit the path that God is moving you through your thinking, attitude, and overall mindset could directly inhibit your ability to deliver your purpose.

Finally, we are back to the defining element of labor: cervical change from a natural perspective and the change of the heart from a spiritual standpoint. Let's talk more about the medical aspect and then we will discuss the spiritual parallel to the believer's heart. Prior to labor, the cervix is between 3-4 centimeters in length, firm, and posterior (rear positioned). It is tightly closed, preventing any passage of the baby into the birth canal before time. In early labor however, the cervix will begin to soften, efface (thin), and dilate (open). As it undergoes these necessary changes, its position also changes. As a result, it transitions from a rear facing position, to mid and finally to an anterior (forward) position. All of these changes are necessary to facilitate the delivery of the baby.

Spiritually, the same thing must occur and does occur when God is preparing to birth forth what He has placed in each believer. Just like the cervix must soften and open to allow the fetus to be expelled; so must the heart of the believer soften and open so God can deliver forth what is in the believer. Just like the cervix in the beginning of pregnancy is firm, similarly the heart of a new believer can remain firm or hardened in their early walk with Christ.

As they begin to crave the Word and experience more of Christ, the heart of man becomes soft and begins to open. Evidence of this is found in Ezekiel 36:26 where God says, "I will give you a new heart and put a new spirit in you; I will remove from you your heart of stone and give you a heart of flesh" (NIV). Flesh is soft, so He is saying, "I will make your heart soft, tender, and yielding." A hardened heart is one that is not submissive and yielding.

A heart that is not submissive and yielding cannot birth forth anything because it is closed! Think about it, in normal pregnancy, the cervix does not begin to open until maturity has been reached. Thus spiritually, when maturity is reached in the believer, the heart of man can now open to release all that God has purposed for it to bring forth. Thus, the initiation of spiritual labor. Similarly, the same way the cervix must be examined to determine if it is dilating (opening), so must the heart of man also be examined for progress.

Progress is monitored throughout the entire phase of labor. I can only determine if a patient is in labor by examining the cervix. When the cervix is open, labor is believed to be in progress. If the cervix is closed, labor is not believed to be in progress. When we believe labor is in progress, the expectation is that the cervix will continue to dilate until it is completely open, allowing delivery of the baby.

Interestingly enough, in first time moms, the cervix will thin first (after softening) and then dilate (open) throughout the labor process. The opposite sequence usually occurs in women who have had multiple pregnancies. In obstetrics, we call the thinning of the cervix "effacement." In actuality, it is the stretching of the cervix which causes it to thin out. This stretching and thinning occurs due to the contractions that are pushing the baby's head up against the cervix. As a result of this constant pressure against the cervix, it thins and dilates. As the cervical change continues throughout labor, the contractions continue to push the baby further down into the birth canal. The cervix must efface 100% in order for a vaginal delivery to be possible.

In all my years of practice, the word "effacement" has always referred to the percentage of cervical thinning that is occurring. Nonetheless, I decided to see what the non-medical definition of effacement meant. What I found, in the Apple online dictionary, is that the word *efface* means to "erase, expunge, blot out, remove, or eliminate." What an epiphany! Effacement is not only imperative and required obstetrically, it is just as crucial spiritually. Think about it. Birth transpires after the stretching, thinning, and opening of the cervix takes place. Until this occurs, birth is not feasible. Likewise, the heart of the believer must also efface in order for God to birth forth what He is developing in them. Effacement in this context does not mean "a thinning" of the heart, but does refer to the need of the heart to have "erased, expunged, removed, or eliminated" things that have negatively impacted the believer's ability to completely love!

Push Vitamin

Your heart must efface in order for God to birth forth what He is developing in you.

Many believers, myself included, have been wounded, hurt, and extremely disappointed by others. As a result, we are challenged with opening our hearts to trust and completely love again. Although understandable, and in many cases justified, the problem still remains that an incompletely dilated heart (like the cervix) cannot birth forth anything. No matter how hard and long you push, nothing will come out. Like the cervix that must be 100% effaced for birth to commence, so too does the heart require 100% effacement to do the same.

In normal labor, cervical effacement does not take place until after the fetus is considered mature. Once this maturity is reached, it is only at that point that the cervix begins to undergo the necessary changes to prepare for delivery. In similar fashion, the ability for the believer's heart to efface *or remove* hurts, wounds, disappointments, fears and so on, is directly related to his or her maturity level. Remember, a mature believer submits readily to the obedience and plan of God. As a result, they are more sensitive to the Spirit of God and readily yield to the power of the Holy Spirit. As the mature believer permits the Holy Spirit to have full control in his life, one of two things occur:

1. The power of the Holy Spirit is able to heal the heart of the believer by expunging/erasing the hurts and wounds of the past, which causes the heart of the believer to increase its dilatation (openness).

Or

2. The power of the Holy Spirit causes the believer's heart to become more trusting and dilated (open) towards God as he or she develops and matures in their spiritual walk, resulting in the believer's ability to eliminate their disappointments and wounds of the past

through the love of God.

1 Corinthians 16:13 says, "Watch, stand fast in the faith, be brave, be strong. Let all that you do be done with love" (NKJV). Commentary regarding this scripture demonstrates that the phrase "be brave" actually means, "play the man." This phrase is said to be emphasizing maturity as opposed to actual bravery. Therefore, what the scripture is really depicting is that as one matures, the ability to perform in love should become evident. This ability is made possible through the power of the Holy Spirit.

Indeed, it is the power of the Holy Spirit which enables the believer to change. Like the cervix requires an internal examination to measure its progress in change, so does the heart of the believer require examination for change. 2 Corinthians 13:5 says "Examine yourselves to see whether you are in the faith; test yourselves. Do you not realize that Christ Jesus is in you—unless, of course, you fail the test?" (NIV). Examinations are mandatory in determining progression, whether examining the heart or the cervix.

> *Examinations are mandatory in determining progression.*

In obstetrics, I am concerned about how well my patient is progressing in labor. Progression is determined by how well the cervix is dilating (opening). I expect the cervix to make a certain amount of change within a specific time frame. When a patient is not progressing appropriately in labor, it is usually a sign that something is wrong. The position of the baby within the birth canal may be misaligned or the baby may be too big to fit through the birth canal. These things are not necessarily faulty, nevertheless they usually result in my patient's inability to push the baby out on her own. Many times, in these situations, she requires a cesarean section.

The spiritual parallel in this is that sometimes what God is developing in you is too big for you to push out on your own. You require a spiritual team to help deliver the gift out of you. Either way, pushing is still necessary. Normal labor requires the patient to push, however a cesarean section requires the team to push down on the patient, to get the baby out. Similarly in life, sometimes we need others to push us through the door that God has opened for us, so that we can manifest His greatness and purpose in us.

Medically, we were discussing progression. I assess if a patient is progressing by how much change took place in comparison to the previous examination I performed. Notice, that *I am* assessing the progression of the patient. The patient is not assessing the progress of herself. Although most women feel different during labor (more pain, pressure, anxiety, etc.), they are not able to determine accurately "how far dilated they are." It's impossible for them to do so because they not only don't know how to do it, but it would also be impossible because they wouldn't know what they are looking for. Same can be true for assessing the heart for progression. The progression of the heart can be measured by the change in the believer's ability to "perform all in love." Yes, there are other changes that have taken place in the believer (behavior, language, desires, etc.) however the ability to perform in love is God's greatest command. Likewise, until the heart is fully dilated to love, one will never have the ability to birth forth His image.

Additionally, it is important that leaders in the Body of Christ (the church) recognize their responsibility to examine the heart of those that God has entrusted to them. If left up to the maturing believer to examine his own heart, or if left to his inability to understand "what" or "how" to check it, he may inaccurately examine it and determine that he is farther ahead or behind than he actually is!

Finally, if left up to someone who may not be as experienced to determine the progress of others, it may be wrongly determined. Remember, this is what happened to me when I presented to the hospital for evaluation. The resident doctor, who is a doctor in training, initially checked me and said I was 2-3 centimeters dilated. It was not until the attending physician, who is an expert in the field, reevaluated her exam, and determined that I was much further ahead than the resident doctor had earlier stated. What is the point? Progress can be misjudged, whether by someone else or we ourselves. As pastors and spiritual leaders, we must be careful who we allow to assess the progress of others in our churches. Likewise, as believers, we too must be mindful of who we allow to assess us, and define our progress.

Progress can be misjudged.

The examination of the heart must involve both the believer and God. Often times, God will use a spiritual leader in the Body of Christ to assist in assessing the believer's progression. As a result, we as leaders must stay in the right posture to hear God so that when we are assessing the progression of those that He has placed in our care, we will be accurate. Nonetheless, it cannot be left alone to the believer to solely determine his own progress. Even Psalm 139: 23-24 says "Search me, Oh God, and know my heart: try me, and know my thoughts: And see if there be any wicked way in me, and lead me in the way everlasting" (NKJV).

Progress is important. Cervical change is good; however, truth be told, as obstetricians, most of us are concerned about whether or not the cervix is opening in a timely fashion. Research performed back in 1955, provided obstetrical data regarding the amount of cervical change that should be evident within a certain time frame. Most obstetricians still use these guidelines to conclude if a woman is or is not progressing well. This is important, because when the cervix is not dilating in a timely fashion, intervention must be considered because this is not normal labor. Intervention may be required if the gift is to be manifested healthy and uncompromised.

Now, this brings me to the need to discuss what is called the Seven Cardinal Movements of Labor that I mentioned earlier. Although these are seven separate position changes that the fetus will move through during the process of labor, they can overlap, with some occurring simultaneously. The baby will undergo these sequential movements in order to pass through the birth canal. If there is a problem with the baby transitioning into one of these discrete movements, the labor process overall can be affected and even hindered. Remember, these movements, although commonly listed in sequential order, can occur at the same time or individually. Additionally, these movements are all in relation to the baby's head as it passes through the birth canal. Let's take a look at each of the labor movements briefly.

Engagement and Descent. These are considered the first two movements the baby will experience upon the commencement of labor. Engagement involves the head of the baby interlocking with the opening of the birth canal. Descent means the head has moved down further in the birth canal. When labor is initiated the head of the baby will move down toward the birth canal and interlock. This demonstrates that the baby is in position and preparing for birth. It is the pressure of the contractions that are moving the baby downward.

Spiritually speaking, we must do the same thing as we prepare to birth our gifts. When the pressures of life arise that are pushing us down closer to the doorway of opportunity God has opened for us, we must submit to the process and engage in His will with our heads first. Why must the head be first? The head is the largest part of the baby's body. Therefore, when it passes through the birth canal first, it is stretching and opening the canal enough so that the entire body can pass through without difficulty, in the normal setting. If feet present first, there is high risk of head entrapment and serious fetal compromise because the feet do not stretch the canal open enough. Therefore, by the time the head reaches the outlet of the vagina, it can become trapped leaving the baby's body hanging on the outside of mom while the head is still caught within the vaginal canal.

In the worst-case scenario, this complication can cause death to baby and harm to the delivering mom. Spiritually, we must move through the process and the pathway God has for us, with our heads down. When we do so, we demonstrate our submission to allowing Christ to be the head and lead us through our purposed path.

Flexion. As the baby is moving through the birth canal, its head will begin to experience resistance from the muscles within the birth canal. Due to this resistance the baby's head will bend toward its chest (flex). Likewise, the process to delivering the purpose and greatness of God to others is not easy. At times, you will encounter resistance. When you do, the key is that you flex your head towards your chest and pray! James 5:16 states, "the earnest prayer of a righteous person has great power and produces wonderful results" (NIV). Another translation I really like says, "The prayer of a righteous person is powerful and effective" (NIV). Resistance can be overcome through the power of prayer.

Internal Rotation. This step is likely occurring with flexion. When labor first starts, the head of the baby, although down, is often turned sideways, with the face and eyes looking to the side. As the baby progresses through this labor movement, its head is forced to rotate downward (sometimes upward). When this occurs, the baby's head has usually reached the widest part of the birth canal and baby is nearing actual delivery.

Spiritually, this movement is interconnected with the previous movement of flexion. Prayer not only has power to overcome the obstacles we face, but it also has the ability to keep us focused. Distractions are always around, causing our heads to often be turned contrary to the direction needed for delivery. It's important to allow the Holy Spirit to keep your eyes on the task at hand. Especially when delivery is just around the corner.

Extension and External Rotation. At the moment the baby's head is delivered, the force of the delivery causes its head to extend upward as the neck bends back. It then externally rotates, meaning the head will align itself with the spine of the baby. This alignment occurs because the pressure and resistance has finally been eliminated. Remember, we are ultimately delivering the Image of Christ to others. As we mentioned earlier, this image may be presented as ministries, books, professional or academic aspirations, community programs, and the like. The image of Christ can also be presented more directly through actual face-to-face interactions. Whether directly or indirectly presented, everything born from the believer should ultimately point upwards. In other words, it should direct others towards God. When this takes place, it demonstrates that what was born is in alignment with the Word of God.

Think about it. We have already said that when God's Word is developing and growing in you; it will cause you to become a new creature in Him. Additionally, this transformation you are personally experiencing by the Word of God, will also give rise to the ability of your greatness, purpose, dreams, and hopes to grow within you. When this purpose is finally birthed, no matter what form it possesses it should represent the image of Christ and point others towards Him. When this occurs, what you birthed will be in alignment with who you are in Christ as a new creature, living a new life.

Expulsion. Once the head is delivered, the shoulders will now move underneath the pubic bone allowing the rest of the baby's body to be expulsed out. The gift is completely out. Likewise, if we follow the plan of God for our lives and allow Him to guide us through the path He has designed for us, He will no doubt eject our purpose completely into the world for others to see and be blessed. Our purpose is God's gift, through us, to others. The key is that we submit to the change He desires to perform within us. If we do not change we cannot progress. Change is necessary.

A certain amount of change should be evident by a certain time in a believer's walk with Christ. When a believer has been saved for a long time, and little or no progression is seen in his life, attitude, behavior, communication, etc.; intervention needs to be considered or implemented, as this is not normal.

Now, when God is softening and dilating the heart of the believer, like contractions, this can be a very painful process because often times it requires us to face painful realities about ourselves and others. Pain is a normal part of labor and it is necessary. Unfortunately, our culture associates just about all pain as being something negative. This is not true in all cases, and definitely is not true in labor. Labor pains are a sign that the body is preparing for the delivery of something great! Labor pains represent the advancement towards the delivery of something very much anticipated. Labor pains are purposed to push out the new creature that has finally matured. Labor pains create the pressure necessary to deliver what lies inside. Labor pains ARE a part of the process!

So, like I tell my laboring patients: STOP fighting against the contractions! Breathe with it, relax in it, and let it do its job. Yes! I know it's easier to say it than to do it, but it's necessary! Often times, when the contractions become stronger, my patients begin to writhe all over the bed. Many yell and scream. Others moan and wail. Like all women experiencing the agony of labor pains, I too have manifested my personal reaction while experiencing the agonizing pains of labor. Yet and still, no matter how painful they were, they were necessary to deliver my three wonderful gifts (my children) into this world. So too, the believer must "endure hardness as a good soldier of Jesus Christ" (2 Timothy 2:3, KJV). When you can continue to overcome your pain through Jesus Christ, and not give up or become weary, then "at the proper time [you] will reap a harvest if [you] do not give up" (Galatians 6:9, NIV).

The agonizing pains of labor are so great that many of us would rather have death. I can only imagine how Christ felt while being crucified in order

Push Vitamin

When you can continue to overcome your pain through Jesus Christ, and not give up or become weary, then at the proper time [you] will reap a harvest if [you] do not give up (Galatians 6:9, NIV).

that He might complete His assignment so that we could have the gift of eternal life. It was His grace that saved us. How wonderful that this grace is demonstrated, in the agony of labor. You may wonder what I mean. Well, stay with me. We agree that labor is painful and causes excruciating pain. With that said, GRACE by way of the epidural is present in our day. This epidural was designed to eliminate the pain and suffering women experience when in labor. It was designed to relieve the tension women of-ten exhibit when experiencing such pain.

Like Christ, although a solution to eliminating the pain or suffering is present, each individual must choose whether she wants it. This is her choice. Needless to say, I have many patients who decline the epidural and choose to continue their process with suffering and pain. Unfortunately, they do not realize that the tension they exhibit in response to their circumstance, is only impeding their progress to deliver what's inside.

When my patients tense up their bodies with a contraction, I often find that the opening of their cervix tends to be hindered. The pelvic muscles are so tense, that the ability for the baby to move down further in the pelvis, and the ability for the cervix to continue dilating, can be negatively impacted in some women. Remember, the purpose of the contractions are to continue to stretch and thin the cervix until it *completely* opens! *Completely*, meaning it has dilated to 10 centimeters. The maximum stretch! In obstetrics, when a laboring patient is fully dilated, or stretched to ten centimeters, we say they are "complete!" *Completely dilated*, indicating that the doorway to the birth canal is fully open and pushing can now commence.

> ## MEN'S PERSPECTIVE
>
> ### Labor Process
>
> **Me:** *How did you feel watching me labor?*
>
> **Greg:** *I felt concerned. I probably didn't know how to respond yet. We were only married a little over one year when we had our first child.*

It was very interesting to me that Greg stated he felt "concerned" because his actions, at the time, did not seem to demonstrate that of concern. In fact, when he first answered the question he responded that he was "very compassionate, concerned, and felt terrible that I had to experience that pain." I was confused by his answer and had to remind him that he was very distracted with fixing a computer at the time I was in the height of my labor. So much so, that he actually left the house, leaving me to labor in agonizing pain. Thank God my mom was present. When he did return, it was late. He got into bed, and went to sleep. I was on the floor alone, struggling with the pain of labor.

For years I resented the fact that Greg was not attentive to the pain I was experiencing. He had always been an attentive and caring man. I couldn't understand why he would leave me at such a critical point. *Didn't he notice I was in pain?*

Although I had let go the hurt long before now, I did not finally receive a full understanding of my husband's behavior towards me until now. As we continued this discussion, reminiscing the events of that night, I prodded for answers. I honestly wanted to know, *why would he leave me at such a painful time?* All of a sudden, during our conversation, he spontaneously answered,

"I seriously felt concern. I probably didn't know how to respond yet. We were only married a little over one year."

When he responded in transparency and honesty "I probably didn't know how to respond yet," I got it!

Naturally and spiritually, you will find that people do not always know how to respond to your hurt and pain. It makes them uncomfortable and uneasy because they don't know how to help you. Although, this can be hurtful to those of us that are wanting and needing help, we must not take it personally. We must realize that some individuals although they may want to help, they can't! Emotionally they are not strong enough. They can love you and support you in other ways. Stress, pain, and grief are a challenge for them. As a result, those of us that are expecting our loved ones, friends, and others to help us in stressful or painful situations, may often feel abandoned. We must not feel this way. They are not abandoning us from a malicious standpoint. It is often out of fear, helplessness, or both.

Greg and I were young and immature at that time of our lives. He had not yet learned how to support someone emotionally in a stressful situation, and I had not yet learned how to give someone the benefit of the doubt. Therefore, he found something else to distract his attention from what he felt he could not control. He is no different from most individuals—whether in church or out. He truly was concerned, but just didn't know *how* to express it. So, he avoided engaging in the situation.

The principle here is to understand that we can often misinterpret the actions of others. We must learn to give people the benefit of the doubt when they fail to support us in our stressful or painful times of need. Likewise, we must be careful that we do not allow unforgiveness to come into our hearts and stifle our process of growth and development.

EIGHT

Time To Push

"You are complete!"

"I gotta push!" The woman screams out!

"I gotta PUUUUUSHHHH! Can I push, pleeeeeeease—I gotta push!"

She tried to obey the instruction "not to push," however, the involuntary contractions of her pelvic and rectal muscles caused her to bear down and push.

It was not her intention to disobey the instruction to avoid pushing, however the urge to push was too great and she had no control over it.

Release and relief is all she desired.

This was my experience during the birth of my first child, Brooke. Talk about pain and pressure. *I will never forget that experience. Yet, I will never regret that experience.* The reality at that time was the massive urge to push! I never realized a pressure could be so great! I never imagined an inability to control my body could be so authentic! Finally, I never understood the act of pushing involved so much!

Up until now, it had not been time to push. In fact, pushing was out of the question because it is medically impossible if my cervix was not fully dilated. To push against a cervix that is not fully open is to risk damage and injury to it. Having an urge and a desire to push doesn't mean it's time to push. In addition to contraction pain, I also felt the urge to push. What many don't realize is that I presented to the hospital two times previous to this visit. Unfortunately, when my cervix was examined, I was only two centimeters on both occasions and discharged to home in early labor. My urge and desire to push did not change the fact that there was a certain time to push. Timing is everything in this obstetrical situation.

Push Vitamin

Having the urge to push doesn't mean it's time to push.

Yes, there are physiological changes occurring in the body during labor and leading one closer to the time to push. Yes. One is able to push when the cervix is fully dilated (open), however it does not mean that it is the *time*! Having the ability to do something does not equate with being the right time to do it. Although, we obstetricians understand this fact, our patients unfortunately do not, as it pertains to pushing. As a result, injuries sometime occur during this stage.

Although a patient *can* start pushing once she has reached

complete dilation, in all my years of practice, I have never had a patient begin to push until I authorized pushing to begin. That's just the way it works. If a nurse examines a patient and finds she is complete, the nurse will notify me, then ask "may we begin pushing." If I am the one who examines the patient's cervix and determines she is complete, then I tell the nurse, "She is complete. Start pushing!" In either case, permission to push must be given. The same thing is needed spiritually. Many of us are pushing who have not received permission to push. From whom does that permission come? I believe it should come from God.

At times, the cervical exam may reveal that the patient's cervix is completely dilated (wide open); however, the baby's position in the pelvis is still very high. The term we use for this in obstetrics is "the head is not engaged." Engaged means, the head of the fetus has interconnected with the entrance to the maternal pelvis (the birth canal). Therefore, "the head is not engaged" means that the head is above the point *(sometimes high above it)* of where it needs to unite with the doorway of the birth canal. Simply put: It is out of position.

The door to the birth canal is open; however, the head of the baby needs to "come down more," as we obstetricians say. To start pushing at this point, although certainly acceptable, usually leads to maternal exhaustion because the patient has to work harder and longer to push the baby's head down through the birth canal. At times, the fetus cannot tolerate long stages of pushing, and as a result its heart rate will demonstrate distress. For this reason we will often let the patient "labor down" before pushing. This involves, sitting the patient straight up and allowing the contractions to continue to push the baby down closer to the maternal pelvis. This is a passive action, because it does not involve the patient using force. Instead it allows the patient's body to do the pushing (*work*) for her. She is simply waiting for her body to assist in the process.

The doorway to the birth canal is already completely open; she just needs time to wait for the fetus to enter it. Once that takes place, pushing can begin with the anticipation of the manifestation that what's within her is to be delivered soon.

The Bible talks about various types of doors all throughout: doors of our lips, doors of hope, ancient doors, doors in general, and of course, Jesus as the Door. There is one particular scripture which, to me, parallels so closely to the obstetrical term, "engagement." It's in 1 Corinthians 16:9 where Paul has written to the Corinthians that "I will tarry in Ephesus until Pentecost, for a great and effective door has been opened to me." Another translation says, "a wide door for effective work has opened unto me" (ESV). What strikes me in this passage of scripture is the fact that Paul states that a door *has already been* opened. He's not waiting for it to open. It's already open. Yet, he still says he "will tarry (wait) in Ephesus." But why? Why wait when the door is already open? He is waiting because it is not yet time for him to go through this door. He was waiting to *engage* this great door of opportunity in the appointed time! For him, it was Pentecost. As we know, when Pentecost came, there was such an amazing outpouring of the Holy Spirit from God to man. This was not only a great and effective work, but a life changing work for all those who experienced this blessing.

Like the cervix, just because it's wide open, doesn't mean it's the appointed time to push, whether the urge is present or not. Similar to Paul, the believer must learn to tarry (wait) for the appointed time patiently, peacefully, and confidently. Knowing that when God's appointed time to push is given, one can push with the confidence that what God will birth out of him or her will not only be great and effective, but like Pentecost, will change the lives of those awaiting.

Waiting is not a bad thing. Similar to my patients, the children of God often struggle to understand the timing to push. Moreover, some believers, like my patients, need to "labor down." In other words, they need to allow their Body to assist them in the birthing process. By Body (notice the word is capitalized), I mean the Body of Christ. The church. When God opens the heart of the mature believer, she begins to trust God more. This trust leads to increased obedience. And obedience allows one to move closer to manifesting the fullness of his or her divine purpose.

Many times in this process, you need the assistance of others to push you toward and through the door of opportunity and destiny. Many times, those trying to push on their own, and before the appointed time, will utilize so much of their own strength, that they become exhausted and can often distress the very life God is trying to birth through them. "Wait on the Lord, and be of good courage. Again,

I say, wait!" (Psalm 27:14). We must learn that the *Kairos* (meaning God appointed time or the right time) moment for delivery is determined by God and is always the right time. Our responsibility is to engage (join) what God is doing in our lives, and the rest will follow if we obey His voice and His instruction pertaining to when to push.

So let's talk about the pushing stage in more detail. Pushing is obviously not easy. As a matter of fact, for my first-time expectant mothers, pushing requires plenty of instructions, coaching, and support. The first thing I want to discuss is the instructions. Once I give the permission to push, either the nurse or myself then begins to give direction regarding *how* to push. These instructions are important because they help facilitate this stage of labor. If one does not correctly push, descent of the baby can be hindered and normal delivery could potentially be prevented.

So how does one push? That depends on where you are delivering and who is delivering you. Honestly! Truth be told, there are many different methods of pushing. There are different positions, techniques, and styles. Some squat, some lay on their side, some lay flat on their back, some push in birthing pools, some sit in birthing chairs, and so on. There are too many to discuss each separately. For that reason, I am only going to concentrate on the essential principles involved in pushing, no matter which method is implemented.

The first principle of pushing is *Support*. Think about it. Women in this country do not generally birth babies alone. When it does happen, it is an extremely rare circumstance and not intended.

When I walk into a delivery room to say, "It's time to push," there is usually a good presence of family and friends who all begin to verbally express extreme excitement at hearing these words. Soon-to-be grandmothers and grandfathers jump up and grab their cameras. Soon-to-be fathers start texting and telling everyone "the baby is about to be here!" Aunties, uncles, and friends begin to pace with joy in anticipation of seeing the new baby. Even in the few situations where a patient of mine does not have anyone who has come to the hospital to be with her, she is still not alone. She is not alone because we, the medical staff (nurses and physicians), are present to experience her birth. Not only are we present, but we are also directly involved in the delivery of this precious gift.

Support system. That's what everyone in the room becomes at the moment pushing begins. I still chuckle today, when I see all the support people get so distracted by the fact that it's time to push, that they forget the reason why they came to the hospital with the patient in the first place. Everyone begins to pull out cell phones and cameras. Some even leave the room to alert others in the waiting room that "pushing "is about to begin.

In the nine years I've been practicing, it never fails, that at this point in the laboring process, I have to remind the support people that they are there to support. At that instance, I begin to assign each individual their role for support. Some are assigned to holding the legs upward during pushing, others are assigned to lifting the patient's shoulders gently; some are given the task of counting while the patient is pushing, and others are assigned the responsibility of keeping the patient focused while pushing. No matter what the assignment, the support is essential. Immediately after the assignments are given, I give detailed instructions regarding how to support the patient properly.

I personally, have never seen a woman push or birth an infant alone. Support has always been present, even if it were just me, the nurse, and the resident. Unfortunately, the Body of Christ, at times has forgotten their need to support those that are laboring and commencing to push forth what God has placed in them. The word support in addition to "carrying," or "lifting," also means "to bear" (Mac Computer Dictionary). To bear one's load requires strength and stability. If you don't believe me, ask someone who has been a "leg holder" for a woman during her pushing stage. I've seen this thousands of times! A contraction begins, and I instruct the "leg lifters" (as I affectionately call them) to pull the legs back. When my patient begins to push, instinctively, she begins to tense up her legs, pushing them outward and against the very ones that are trying to hold them back.

Although it's not her intent, she begins fighting against those who are there to support her. I've watched "leg lifters" stumble slightly, sweat, and change their stances in an effort to hold the patient's legs steady and in position. I have also had individuals who requested someone else to hold up the legs because they themselves were tired and needed a break. Some have even quit all together.

Who in the Body of Christ will hold up the legs of the believer who is in the pushing process? Where are the "strong who ought to bear with the failings of the weak and not to please ourselves" (Romans 15:1, NKJV)? Many may not realize that the reason we ask others to hold up the patient's legs is because in most cases, we want to prevent the patient from getting tired too quickly or the patient is already too weak or tired to do it herself. Thus the need for support. Spiritually speaking, we need leg lifters to help carry the weight while others are actively pushing. This can be demonstrated by actively helping someone. Give your time, your skill, or your talent. Basically give yourself, physically, to help. Ask what you can do to assist. Volunteer your time, if needed. Whatever you can do, just help lift the weight. Galatians 6:2 says, "Share each other's burdens, and in this way [you] obey the law of Christ" (NLV).

Finally, lifting the legs upward while pushing is important because it also opens up the pelvis and creates more space for the baby. We must realize, that although someone may seem close to delivering, while they are yet pushing, we need to help them "open up more" (emotionally and/or spiritually). By this I mean, creating more room within their heart and spirit whereby via the anointing of the Holy Spirit he or she can push out the purpose of God for their life. Pushing can cause people to become nervous, fearful, weary, and doubtful. Doubt is something I see quite often because the process of pushing often takes a lot longer than patients expect.

In actuality, patients can push up to three hours with an epidural and up to two hours without. As a result, patients, out of frustration and exhaustion, begin to say aloud "I can't do it." It is at that moment that it becomes my responsibility to "open her mindset and emotions" through encouragement. I remind her of how strong she is. I remind her that we are here to do this together. Through my words, I "lift" her mental weight and burden that's attempting to inhibit the progress. In life, we must learn to encourage each other. We seem to struggle with this. Additionally, we must learn to encourage ourselves at times that others will not, or are not available to, do so.

Now then, this leads me to the next principle: *Position*. As I mentioned earlier, there are many different types of positions. However, what is important to realize about position, is that it requires the support of others for it to be maintained. It's the support system of the patient that is responsible for keeping her in the correct position. The patient's position can either assist or hinder the pushing process. Although most obstetricians still position patients on their back while pushing, research has demonstrated that this can actually be counterproductive and more difficult for the patient. Additionally studies have shown that this position decreases the pelvic space, as well as can cause back, hip, and leg injuries from the pressure exerted on these particular body parts while pushing. Honestly, speaking, this position is still used today out of convenience. It is easier for the physician and staff delivering.

Other pushing positions have been examined, and found to increase pelvic space, minimize tearing, shorten time to delivery, decrease use of extra maternal strength, and prevent bodily injury. Wow! If the Body of Christ could grasp the importance of support, in relationship to position, we would have less emotional, spiritual, and sometimes physical injuries in the Body of Christ. Additionally, believers active in the process of trying to push out the gift that God has placed within them may have an easier time delivering, with fewer wounds. Finally, believers must be careful that they do not let others place them in a position simply out of convenience. Especially when it definitely works against the efforts of what God is trying to do. Position should not be compromised for any reason. When believers are in any position other than where God has instructed them to be, blessings are bound to be missed.

Position is important as it pertains to the delivery and receipt of a blessing. Malachi 3:10, reveals this fact. Although, Malachi is talking about the principle of tithing, something more interesting regarding position has always struck me with this verse. After God gives instructions regarding what to do with the tithes, He then challenges the believer to "prove Him now" and see if He won't "open to you the windows of heaven, and pour out for you such blessing, that *there will* not *be room* enough *to receive it*" (NKJV). At first glance, one may not understand *what* this scripture has to do with the principle of *position*. However, for years I have used this scripture to preach the importance of position as it pertains to receiving blessings.

Most individuals simply focus on the fact that if we as believers are obedient, God will pour out so much blessing that we will not be able to receive it! Now that's awesome; however, receiving a blessing so abundant is just part of it! When I look at this scripture, my focus is on the opening of the windows of heaven, and a pouring out of a blessing. When you look deeper at this scripture, it is clear that there is a specific position needed in order to receive the blessing. Yes! A blessing is being poured out, but from where is it being poured? The window of heaven. Therefore, it is clear that in order to receive the blessing, you must be *under the window*. If you are positioned anywhere else, you will not receive this blessing. It's like what we were just talking about regarding pushing when the fetal head is not in the correct position; it can delay the process and progress of delivery. Pushing is longer and harder, therefore hindering the time of manifestation regarding the blessing inside of the believer.

This same principle holds true for those preparing to push in The Kingdom of God. When one is out of position, it can cause the blessing of the Lord to not be readily available to those purposed to receive it. Think about it, when there's a delay in pushing, it prolongs the waiting time for the family, friends, etc. to see the anticipated baby. Spiritually this works the same. When those birthing forth the things of God are out of position, those that God has designed to receive what is about to be delivered will miss the divine blessing intended for them to experience.

Now the final principle of pushing: *Focus*. During the pushing process, I am constantly reminding my patients to focus. This is needed because pushing not only requires a significant amount of physical exertion, but it can also be a very painful process. I say it *can* be painful, because some women may not experience much pain at all, especially those that have received an epidural. Nevertheless, either situation still requires focus.

Pain can make people act and speak in ways they never would have imagined. Pain can distract people. Pain can make individuals want to give up. Pain can cause people to move or not move. Pain can change one's mood or attitude, and pain can produce fear. Indeed, pain can cause people to lose focus.

Labor pain is a good pain. It is a much-needed pain. Why? Because this pain is producing the manifestation of something great! This pain is literally helping to squeeze out the blessing of life. This pain is generating the necessary pressure to push forth the things of God from the expectant believer. Without this pressure, patients in labor do not know when to push. I am always instructing my patients to "push when you have a contraction." To push outside of contraction pain is not recommended. Timing during the pushing process is very important. Many obstetricians (including myself) believe that pushing should only be initiated at the time a contraction is occurring, whether it's painful or not. When pain is present, we instruct our patients to "push through the pain!" This approach is called directed pushing. Other physicians may instruct patients to push only when they feel like their body is directing them to do so. This is called spontaneous pushing.

Whether directed or spontaneous pushing, they both require focus. I have noticed many times with my patients experiencing painful contractions, that if they focus on the pain more than the task at hand, they become ineffective at pushing. Their mindset begins to deteriorate as they begin to succumb to the severity of the pain and tell themselves that they "cannot do it." They begin to struggle with maintaining their position. They begin to fight against the very ones trying to support them. Some curse, some yell, some flail around. It is at this time, I stop the entire pushing process and command the mother to FOCUS! Yes! Looking right in her eyes, I proclaim firmly that actual word.

After commanding focus, I tell my patient "You can do this. We are a team. I need you to help me do this. Push through the pain. You are doing great. You are strong and will get through this. STAY FOCUSED!" When focus is lacking, it becomes difficult to complete the birthing process. This difficulty does not just affect the patient, but it also becomes difficult for those who are assigned to support her through this process. This difficulty arises when the patient becomes unwilling to listen, and follow instructions. At times those present to support can become offended by the very words directed towards them by those pushing.

Ironically, the children of God, who are in the process of pushing, can also demonstrate the same behavior when lacking focus. Lack of focus, can result in fear. Lack of focus, can transform a positive thinking mind into one of negativity. Lack of focus, can cause people to give up. Lack of focus, gives way to distraction. And finally, lack of focus can cause offenses.

When the Children of God lack focus, their assigned tasks

become delayed and potentially in jeopardy. The Bible says, "As a [man] thinketh in his heart, so is he" (Proverbs 23:7, NKJV). If you allow the pains of the past and present to tell you that you can't accomplish a God directed task, then you will not accomplish it. If you let the lack of focus cause fear to walk through its door then your dismayed mindset will result in your inability to recognize the presence of God with you. This mindset, unfortunately, prevents the Lord from strengthening, helping, and upholding you (Isaiah 50:7), and results in a failure that God had never intended nor purposed for you to experience. Children of God STAY FOCUSED! "Let your eyes look directly forward, and your gaze be straight before you" (Proverbs 4:25, ESV). Remember, that "[you] can do all things through Christ who strengthens [you]" (Philippians 4:13, NKJV)! "Set [your] face like a flint, and know that [you] shall not be put to shame" (Isaiah 50:7, NIV)! Tell yourself that you will not be overcome by the pain and the pressure you are experiencing. BEAR DOWN AND PUSH knowing that if you endure to the end you will prevail.

As I tell my patients, "Take a deep breath. Fill your lungs with air. Curl around your baby (positioning). Bear down and push! When the lungs are filled with air right before pushing commences, this gives the patient the needed force behind the push! Remember, Pneuma is the breath of the Holy Spirit. Therefore, Children of God, when you are commencing to push, you will need the indwelling of the Pneuma (Holy Spirit) to give you the needed power to push and deliver the things of God within you. When God "breathed into Adam's nostrils, the Bible says, "he became a living being" (Gen 2:7, NKJV). This scripture is evidence that the Pneuma of God (the Holy Spirit) will produce life—even that which the believer is birthing forth himself.

Even if pain is not experienced in one's pushing process due to grace (the epidural), the process still requires a tremendous amount of physical exertion, strength, and stress which can still produce fatigue and the desire to give up. Although understandable, whatever it takes, I encourage you, like I do my patients, to stay focused! It is imperative.

The potential for injury is increased when focus is not present. Allow your support people to encourage you and uphold you through this process. Don't fight against them. Don't hurt them. Don't make them work harder than they should. Keep your ears open to hear instructions from God and others He places to speak into your life. Listen to the one who is guiding you through the process. Commit to the process and keep the focus to complete the task. Keep pushing! You are nearing the time to deliver.

> ### MEN'S PERSPECTIVE
>
> #### *Time To Push*
>
> **Me:** *How did you feel when you heard the words "It's time to push?"*
>
> **Greg:** *Those words represented the beginning of the end of the long ten months. I felt like finally! It's here. No more waiting.*

Greg's answer at first glance looked like he was expressing the relief of getting to the end. However, when I looked closer at his answer, he demonstrated an understanding of pushing that is so profound. You see, what Greg conveyed was his understanding that pushing out the gift is not the end all. In fact, it is the beginning of a very different responsibility and a very different life. Yes! We celebrate the fact that what we have been anticipating and expecting to arrive is almost here. The wait *is* almost over, however the work is about to begin.

Many times, we look over the fact that what God is entrusting us with, requires post care and stewardship after it's pushed out. Maintaining the gift, although rewarding, can be challenging, and at times, extremely difficult. Yet, when we realize that work will be needed to sustain what we are about to push out, we can be better prepared to do so. God is always with us to give us the strength, and the knowledge to manage what we are about to deliver.

Nine

The Delivery

It's time to deliver! Oh how I love delivering babies! It's such a wonderful experience in the absence of complications. The anticipation of waiting to see what has been developing inside is over! The gift is finally tangible! It's manifested! It's reality! The pain, the pressure, and the stretching was worth it all. The evidence of one's ability to produce something great has been revealed. The victory in pushing has been received. The ability to produce is genuine, if we trust God. And His purpose has finally been fulfilled.

The head of the baby begins to crown, meaning that the baby's head is now beginning to manifest itself through the vaginal opening with each contraction and push. It is now time to directly prepare for delivery. At this moment, I command the mother to stop pushing, so that I can prepare myself to deliver. I instruct the nurse to "break the bed down!" I begin putting on my sterile gown, gloves, and my blue booties. I roll the delivery table closer to me, so that nothing needed is out of my reach. The patient's legs have been placed in stirrups in order to position them for pushing. Her legs are wide open, and I position myself in between them to receive what is coming forth. Delivery always requires someone to "catch" or "receive" what is being pushed out. Failure to have someone present and in position to receive the baby could result in injury to the baby.

Once gowned up, I prepare myself further for the delivery of this precious gift. I ensure that all anticipated instruments, sponges, etc. are present and readily available when needed. I request soap and water and begin cleaning the vaginal outlet. Finally, I verify that everyone needing to be present for the delivery is in the room and ready to go. Once this is confirmed, pushing resumes.

Pushing in this stage often produces a different type of pain. The patient begins to complain of moderate "burning and stinging" that is very uncomfortable. I reassure her that this is normal because baby's head is stretching the perineum and the vaginal opening. Although, it hurts, I encourage her to stay focused—allowing the head to stretch the tissues in this area will minimize tears. The head continues to emerge. In the final moments leading up to delivery, I request the oil, *mineral oil that is.* The nurse pours it onto the perineum and I begin to massage it around the opening of the vagina. *This will help to decrease the extent of lacerations that may develop.* Finally, I position my hands to support the perineum and receive this gift from God. I am ready, knowing that my anointed hands will be the first to touch and bless this new creature preparing to enter the world for the first time. Pushing continues. More and more of the head emerges until it is out! Finally, the fullness of the gift has been manifested to all. Shouting and yelling usually erupt in the room, as the receipt of the gift is celebrated.

Birth is such a wonderful and beautiful experience! I love to deliver these tiny new creatures into the world! They are truly gifts from God. Similarly, I feel the same way about the spiritual births I have had the pleasure of being a part of, as a pastor. And just like in the natural, these spiritual births are just as wonderful and beautiful. They too need to be and should be celebrated upon their entrance into the world.

Honestly, there is so much medical-spiritual parallel regarding the actual delivery of the baby. For instance, as the believer continues to obey the voice of God regarding when to hold and when to push, the gift within begins to become more visible. Although the believer is becoming closer to the full manifestation of what lies within him or her, there is still an uncomfortable stretching that often takes place. It is during this stretching that I often believe God is providing the room to birth forth the gift inside in hopes of eliminating injury to the soul and spirit of the patient.

Stretching is painful. Ask anyone who has had to endure a fitness class. Nevertheless, God is producing maximum stretch

Stretching is painful, even when God does it.

within the believer, and He is also the one who is actively delivering the gift from within. As the Deliverer, He too has prepared a table in the presence of the room for the believer. He has everything needed to deliver this precious gift. This is so because His table contains the Body of Christ. And it is through Christ that every need is met. Therefore, everything needed to deliver what's in the believer is present and readily available on the Table (Christ).

Finally, I mentioned that I often request oil to be poured onto the vaginal outlet as the baby's head is being delivered. I then massage this oil around the birth outlet. When God is birthing forth His gift from the believer, He often puts His seal on it, so that man will know it is Him. The seal of God is Christ. Christ in the Greek is "Christos." This word is derived from the Greek word Chrio that means "to anoint or smear." It is representative of anything that is smeared, anointed or even poured.

Anytime God is manifesting His gifts in the earth, it must always be sealed with the oil of Christ to verify that it is of God. Once smeared with the oil, the image will always reflect Christ, because He is the anointed. So it is with the believer who is actively birthing forth what is within himself. If truly from God, the gift birthed will reflect the image of Christ because God has already identified it as His with His oil. As God pours His oil upon what we are manifesting, it becomes anointed. And whatever God anoints, He blesses. This gift will not only be a blessing to the individual birthing it forth, but also to those who will encounter its presence.

Like my hands, which are there to support and guide the head of the baby from the vaginal outlet. So is the Hand of God present to support and deliver the things He has placed within each and every believer. That is the beauty of spiritual birth. God is always the delivering physician. In contrast to the way obstetrics is commonly practiced today, God is always on call for His deliveries. In order to fully understand the significance of this fact, one must first understand the common practice in obstetrics as it pertains to delivering laboring patients.

In past years, there used to be one doctor residing within a particular town or community responsible for providing all of the care to the local townsmen and women. As a result, when women were laboring, it was this same doctor who would be present for each delivery. Over the years, the field of obstetrics has evolved from having mostly solo practitioners, to what we now call group practices. Additionally, larger obstetrical practices containing three or more OB/Gyn providers were developed and provided the same type of on-call coverage. The only difference is that the providers all worked for the same medical practice. The purpose of the on-call groups were to improve the quality of life for the physicians. It allowed them more time for adequate rest and time with family.

Although on-call group coverage solved one problem for obstetricians, it formed another for their patients. The problem is that although a patient may have a primary obstetrician who sees her throughout her prenatal care in the office, when time comes that she goes into spontaneous labor, she has no idea who will deliver her until her arrival at the hospital. Well with God, there are no surprises! The believer never has to wonder who will be the primary physician in charge of her birth. In every spiritual pregnancy, God is always the great physician who will be on call to deliver. And, just like I have a specific team present to deliver every child that is birthed into the world, so does our Father God.

Indeed, delivery of a baby requires a team: the obstetrician, the Labor and Delivery nurse, the baby nurse, and sometimes staff from the Neonatal Intensive Care Unit (NICU) team. In all my years of practicing, I have never delivered a baby without a team present. The team is extremely important! Why? Because everyone on the team has a specific role that will commence once the baby has been delivered. We already know that it is the physician who will deliver the baby. And throughout the delivery process, as the obstetrician, I am responsible for managing the care of both the mom and the baby. However, once the baby is delivered, my role to the baby changes. My focus is no longer on baby. The delivery nurse now has the role of focusing on the baby, in addition to the new mom. At times she may be required to assist the physician in the post-delivery care of the patient.

The baby requires a different type of care, for which I am no longer responsible. It is the Pediatric or NICU team that now assumes the responsibility of providing immediate care to the newborn. My job is to focus on mom and the aftermath of the delivery on her body, not on the baby. My job is to repair injury or damage caused by the delivery, and to ensure that the life of the mother is not compromised by the delivery of this wonderful gift, especially since it will be mom's responsibility to take the baby home and provide its stewardship. When God facilitates a delivery, He too does so with a team. Although His team will always include Jesus Christ and the Holy Spirit, it also includes those of us that the Lord has placed in leadership positions within the Kingdom of God.

Many don't understand that only a select group of individuals are present for a delivery (nurse, physician, residents, and students). Moreover, anyone who is present must be authorized. No one else can be there, regardless of his or her desire to be present. Many hospitals have Labor and Delivery policies regarding how many individuals can be in the room for a delivery (this pertains to non-medical individuals). This policy must be heeded despite how many guests the patient may want to be present in the room with her. Several times throughout my career, I have had the opportunity to witness a patient's frustration because she wanted an extra person to stay in the room with her. Despite reminding the patient about the hospital policy, she persists that this person "cannot miss" the delivery and needs to be present.

Indeed, some expectant mothers will say anything in an attempt to persuade us to let a person stay to see their delivery. Other times, I have had unauthorized guests of my patient's refuse to leave, despite reaching the maximum occupants that are allowed in the room. Rarely, but it has happened, security has been called to Labor and Delivery to escort these guest out of the room. Although not a comfortable situation, it was necessary.

So what's the point of all this? Over the years, I have learned that sometimes people have a preconceived idea regarding how their gift (newborn baby) is going to be delivered. More specifically, they anticipate that their gift is going to be delivered amongst a great multitude of people. With that said, sometimes only myself, as the physician, and a nurse were there to receive the gift: others didn't make it, couldn't make, chose not to make it, or as mentioned previously, were excused from being in the room (due to a complication or they were unauthorized).

Interestingly, reread the account of Jesus' birth in The Bible (Luke, Chapter 2 & Matthew 1:18-25). Nowhere will you find any mention that anyone was present with Mary during her delivery of Jesus Christ. There is no mention of friends, family, or midwife being present. Interestingly, the scripture does not even demonstrate that her beloved husband was present; yet we assume he was. I too believe that he was likely present and possibly the only one. Who would have ever imagined that the biggest gift to the world would be delivered at a time that no one else was present to receive it. This is the reality: sometimes what God is birthing out of you will be at a time where no one is there to receive it. Yet it doesn't change the fact that what He birthed out of you is anointed

Push Vitamin

Understand the reality that: sometimes what God is birthing out of you will be at a time where no one is there to receive it.

and purposed for the world.

As believers, we must stop trying to control who should be present to receive our gift. In contrast to obstetrics, God will determine that. We must understand that birth is always in the presence of a limited amount of individuals. It is not until a woman leaves the hospital, returns to her community and begins to alert everyone that "I had the baby," do the masses begin to show up to see, receive, and experience the love of her new baby. Remember, a similar situation occurred with Christ. At birth, those present to receive Him were extremely limited, however, once the announcement went forth that Christ was born, others came to see Him, receive Him, and experience His love.

The important message here is that what God delivers, He also announces! And when His proclamation goes forth that His gift has come forth, one can be assured that what is birthed will accomplish everything it was intended to fulfill. We must trust that God births nothing without a purpose. The journey of every gift, once delivered, is to discover and fulfill its purpose. Fulfillment of the purpose is always successful if the believer stewards the gift under the direction of the Holy Spirit from the time it is birthed, until its appointed time to die.

MEN'S PERSPECTIVE

Delivery

Me: *How did you feel watching the delivery of your children?*

Greg: *Nervous and excited. If you remember, by the time Morgan (our second child) came, I was videotaping. Caleb was exciting because I finally got a little dude to balance the tide.*

Greg expressed many emotions regarding watching the delivery of each of our children. I remember his response to each one, as they were all different. For Brooke, our first daughter he was shocked and without words. He had not anticipated what a delivery would encompass. He was not prepared for what he saw. Brooke was born covered with meconium (fetal bowel movement). It was from the stress of the labor that caused some stress to her. Remember, I labored at home with little support. The increased stress, also stressed the gift.

For Morgan, Greg's response was one of fascination. He had experienced one birth already, and was now more comfortable with the process. This comfort, allowed him to enjoy the delivery. He was able to anticipate things better. He was standing up with his video camera taping everything. Yes! I mean everything. He was like a reporter excited to show the world what we had manifested together. For our last child, Caleb, Greg was absolutely excited. It was our first boy. As a matter of fact, it was the first boy in four generations on my mother's side of the family. The excitement from Greg was that we were delivering something different.

Spiritually, the same can occur. We may find ourselves with different emotions as God begins to birth several gifts out of us over our total life span. Some deliveries may be harder and take more out of us than expected. These deliveries may result in a feeling of relief and exhaustion upon completion of the delivery. Immediately after the delivery, there may be an inability to appreciate what has been birthed due to the physical or emotional stress from which one needs to recover. Other deliveries may be filled with joy and anticipation of something different that will be birthed and received. Sometimes the excitement, can be simply because the season of being patient is over. Whatever the response, we must understand that emotions are normal and expected, whether natural or spiritual, after a delivery.

God created emotions and we must not be afraid to express them. The only thing God desires is that we express them in a Godly fashion, not in a way that will hurt others or ourselves. It's okay to be nervous. Being nervous, doesn't always equate losing trust in God. There is a good nervousness that is simply due to the anticipation of the greatness that is about to manifest.

I love the fact that God has given us the ability to express emotions. Delivering greatness, purpose, hopes and dreams will always involve the expression of our emotions. This is normal and needed.

Ten

The Assessment

EXAMINATION OF WHAT IS DELIVERED

The baby is out! Friends and family who've been present in the room awaiting the manifestation of this wonderful gift, gather around the bed, staring in fascination at the tiny life-filled creature. Tears are flowing, laughter is expelled, and relief is springing forth throughout the room. Attention to mom has come to an abrupt halt by her loved ones. All eyes are now marveling in amazement at the new addition to the family. Pictures are taken, and videos are made of the miracle that lies before them. The new parents begin to assess superficial characteristics of their new baby, while the medical staff begins a more in depth assessment concerning the immediate health and wellness of the new arrival.

T he baby has been delivered. It takes its first breath of life, and begins to cry loudly. The announcement "It's a girl!" or "It's a boy!" goes forth. The room lights up with verbal expressions of hope, happiness, and relief. Tears of joy flow from the face of the vessel that has just delivered this awesome gift of life. It is contagious. And many begin to cry along with her. Immediately, baby is placed on mommy's chest. Skin-to-skin contact is important so that bonding can begin to form between her and baby.

My role has changed. I am no longer responsible for managing the health of the gift. Others, with the expertise to manage the care of newborns, take over as the baby is handed off to that specific team for assessment. I am now focused on assessing if there has been injury to mom's body during the delivery of this gift. During the time that I begin to examine my patient, the assessment of the baby also begins by the team. All awhile the family begins to discuss "who the baby looks like." Nose, ears, cheeks, lips. All are compared to other family members to see who the child might favor. The new parents are eager to determine if the baby looks more like mommy or daddy.

At times, the mommies and daddies express concern regarding the shape of the baby's head. Many convey that it often appears pointed and "like a cone head." I explain to them that this is normal and is due to the baby passing through the birth canal. It's not permanent and will usually resolve within a few days after birth. In obstetrics, the term is called "molding." Molding is the process in which the baby's head is "shaped" (molded) as it passes through the birth canal. This is what allows the baby's head to fit through the narrow passageway of the birth canal. It can only occur because the skull bones of the infant are soft and pliable.

While excitement is being expressed by the new parents, and questions are being answered, a more official health assessment of the baby is already underway by the nurses. The baby must be watched closely as transition from inside of the womb to the outside world can be difficult. Sometimes this difficulty manifests immediately, and other times it occurs later. As a result, a pediatrician is assigned to monitoring the baby throughout its hospital stay. The goal is to ensure that what was delivered is healthy. This is determined only by examination.

So what is the believer spiritually birthing? Throughout my life, I've heard preachers all around the country instructing believers to "push out their blessing!" "Push out the purpose of God!" "Push out your ministry!" and "Push out the promises of God."

As a result, I believe that the Body of Christ is confused as to what is truly being delivered from within the believer. Remember, it is the Word (Christ the Seed) that has united with the believer's mature seed of faith during conception. Once the two have united together, they become one and implant within the heart of the believer where they begin to multiply and grow. Provided the believer has followed all of God's instructions throughout his or her spiritual "prenatal course," and maintained a healthy spiritual pregnancy, there should be no question regarding "What it is that's being delivered? Or who it looks like?"

Similar to natural delivery, the same question must be answered after a spiritual delivery. What is it? and Who does it look like or resemble? Regarding What is it? We know from a spiritual aspect that what is birthed will not be a boy or girl! What it should and will be, in the presence of a normal spiritual pregnancy that has not been compromised in any way, is the image of God's Son! Stay with me and I'll explain. This is evident in Romans 8:29 which states, "for those whom he foreknew he also predestined to be conformed to the image of His Son..." Yes, all throughout the pregnancy, what should be developing inside the believer is the image of God's Son.

The image of God's Son is multifaceted. Birthing forth the image of God's Son in the earth means we should be delivering Love, Peace, Healing, Hope, and Salvation, amongst other things. Therefore, there should be no problem answering the question, whom does this gift look like after spiritual birth takes place? Spiritually speaking, what is delivered should ultimately look like Christ! Whether its ultimate manifestation is in the form of a ministry, a book, a business, or other, it should ultimately reflect qualities of Christ. Furthermore, like a newborn baby, whose looks and features are being compared to its mom, dad, or others in the family, so should the features of Christ be manifested clearly in what has just been birthed.

Push Vitamin

What you deliver should ultimately reflect the qualities of Christ.

Evidence of molding should also be visible. Spiritually, this confirms that the mind (the head) has been reshaped into the mindset of God. This serves as evidence that the gift has been transformed into the likeness of God. To determine this, a post-delivery assessment must be performed.

We in the Body of Christ often look at our gifts like they belong to us and are akin to material possessions. We forget that these gifts of purpose, greatness, and talents ultimately belong to God. He is simply entrusting us to steward them well during our lifetime. We must not forget that the greatness and purpose inside of us should not only be the image of Christ; but this greatness and purpose is life. Remember, Christ is Life. Therefore what we manifest into the earth should bring life to others. More specifically it should draw people towards the love of Christ, in hopes that they too through your gift will come to know Him, and choose to enter into relationship with Him.

The APGAR TEST

The APGAR Test is a scoring system that is assigned to various characteristics of the baby at 1 minute and 5 minutes of life. This assessment begins immediately after the baby is born. Each letter of the word APGAR represents what specifically is assessed in the baby:

- A – Activity (muscle tone)
- P – Pulse rate
- G – Grimace (reflex)

- A – Appearance (skin color)
- R – Respirations

All of these conditions are assessed to determine the immediate health of the baby. The muscle tone of the baby is evaluated and scored to determine the *Activity* of the baby. This assessment involves evaluating if the baby is moving vigorously or is the baby limp? *Pulse* or heart rate, is also an important assessment because if there is no heartbeat, then the life of the baby is in jeopardy. Likewise, it is the same with *Respirations*, another characteristic assessed immediately after baby is born. If the respiratory effort is low, then that means the baby is not breathing well and may need oxygenation. The *Appearance* of the baby is evaluated by assessing the color of the baby's skin. If blue, it's a sign the baby is not getting enough oxygen and may be in distress. If skin color is pink, it confirms that good blood flow is moving throughout the body of the newborn baby. Finally *Grimace*. This assesses the reflex when the baby's airway is stimulated.

I firmly believe that assessments of the spiritual gifts need to be performed in the Body of Christ. And like the APGAR test we use to assess the immediate health of our newborn babies, I am convinced that we should be utilizing this same type of assessment (in a spiritual sense) in the Body of Christ. In the remaining part of this chapter, I have outlined and explained each assessed characteristic of the APGAR test and demonstrated how I believe it should be used to examine what believers everywhere in the Kingdom of God are birthing forth. So let the assessment begin!

A – Activity (muscle tone)

As leaders in the Kingdom of God, we should be assessing the activity of the gift that is birthed forth from each and every believer. I mentioned earlier that what each believer should be birthing should be the image of Christ in the earth. The bottom line is simply that Christ represents Life! And when an individual has an initial encounter with Christ that results in him or her being born again, they now have new Life. If Christ is Life and we, as believers, are His image in the earth, then that means every believer should be delivering the Gift of Life (Christ) to the world.

So let's assess your gift. Is it active? Or is it limp? What is the tone of your gift? Remember, Christ was active. He was never stationary, and was always on the move to take the Word to the masses. He traveled afar to bring life to those that would hear it, accept it, believe it, and live it. Our gifts should be no different. It amazes me, how many believers are delivering a stagnant Word inside and outside the Body of Christ. Of course we know that The Word itself is not stagnant. The problem is that the individuals delivering the Word have made it stagnant because of how they present it. It is limp because we have allowed ourselves to become weary and tired in purpose.

We go through our entire spiritual pregnancy journey, birth forth what God intended, begin stewarding the gift with excellence, and then somewhere along the way lose momentum. Some get lazy, or distracted. Others' gifts become limp, due to fear. Additionally, the Activity of our gift can be compromised by our procrastination. As a result, the believer fails to keep active what God intended to keep moving.

P – Pulse

This is heart rate. It signifies life and that something or someone is living. This assessment is extremely important after baby is born because it reveals whether the life of the baby is in jeopardy, and whether or not intervention is needed. Similar to the natural, we must spiritually assess the heart rate of what is spiritually birthed. In other words we need to assess whether or not it has life. Same idea holds true when the believer has delivered. We need to assess if it is living! Jesus said, "I am the Way, the Truth, and the Life" (John 14:6, NKJV). He also said, "I came that [you] may have Life and that more abundantly" (John 10:10, NKJV).

Therefore if Christ is Life and He came to bring Life, why is life not visible in what some are birthing forth? Where is its heartbeat? Even more challenging is this question: "Is Life undetected because it's not being presented?" And, why don't we see life being manifested through our gifts and into our churches, communities, jobs, and family, on a consistent basis? Could it be that the earth is lacking in its ability to see and experience true Life through the gift of the believer because we have removed its very Life?

Perhaps we have removed its life because we present the Word to others on a plate of doubt. We present the Word on a plate of unforgiveness. Or worse, we present The Word on a plate of condemnation. We are harsh in judging the very ones that we have been called to minister. As a result, many have left the church and have no desire to return. They are wounded or angry and feel that the church is a hypocrite. They do not see, nor feel the love of Christ, and they question whether what we teach is true, since we sometimes struggle to manifest it properly ourselves. Unfortunately, where Christ is not visible, Life is not visible. As a result, no heartbeat can be detected. Where Christ is partially visible, a weak heartbeat will be detected. Either one inhibits the ability for others to completely see and come to know Christ in His fullness.

G - Grimace

This is also called reflex irritability. The purpose of this test is to assess how the baby responds to stimuli. Normally, to evaluate this characteristic, the nurse will either tap the bottom of the baby's feet or rub the baby's back vigorously. When a more invasive suction device has to be placed down the nostrils of the baby to clear the lungs, this same characteristic can also be analyzed. The baby's response is scored. Scoring is provided based on the following observation after the stimulation was given:

1). No response to the stimuli

2). Some response to the stimuli which is manifested as facial movement only (a grimace)

3). Active response to the stimuli manifested as crying, coughing, sneezing (airway response), or the baby actively pulling away from the stimulation.

So, once again, this brings me to the spiritual aspect. When the gift of the believer is touched by others, "How does it respond?" Maybe the question to ask is whether there even is a response. I'm not talking about touching in the form of attacking. I'm referring to the genuine faith-filled touches that individuals will reach out to give to the Kingdom-birthed gifts in hopes of receiving wholeness, healing, peace, deliverance, forgiveness, joy, etc. When the woman with the "issue of blood" reached out to touch the Gift (Jesus), He actively responded. He did not keep moving (no response) and He did not simply smile or frown (grimace) and continue walking away. No! He actively responded by turning around and speaking (activation of his airway). Not only did He speak, but He spoke with concern, sincerity, and love. In reflecting the image of Christ we should be responding to others with the same characteristics.

MEN'S PERSPECTIVE

Assessment of What's Delivered

Me: *How did you assess each child immediately after their birth? What were you looking for?*

Greg: *I made an assessment prior to birth. You always want your children to receive the best and exceed your current situation.*

Me: *This is the after birth assessment, when you took your first look at the baby.*

Greg: *Ok. But you still make assessments during birth. But yes, they exceeded my expectations and I assessed them as unstoppable.*

Me: *You assessed them as exceeding your expectation? Tell me more.*

Greg: *They were more beautiful than I imagined. Bigger than I thought they would be. And more precious than I knew they could be.*

Me: *How did you assess they were unstoppable, just by looking at them? I need you to go back to that moment.*

Greg: *They looked strong, and I determined that they would grow to be able to do whatever they set out to do.*

Me: *Is it something the babies did that made you determine they were strong or did they simply look strong and unstoppable?*

Greg: *Simply looked.*

Honestly, I was lost when Greg first responded to the question. I felt he misunderstood what I was asking. Making an assessment prior to birth? What kind of answer is that? It was not until I really paid attention to what he was saying, did it make sense. You always want your children to receive the best and exceed your current situation. Aha! I understood what he was saying.

You see, psychologists talk about present-focused, past-focused, and future-focused individuals. These are personality traits different individuals are believed to possess. Present-focused individuals focus on the "right now." They focus on the task at hand and do a good job with that task. They are more short-term focused and like instant gratification. Past-focused individuals focus on past experiences, dates, events, etc. They are excellent when it comes to detailing events of the past, but believe the quality of their past will determine their future. Future-focused individuals are often long-term oriented. They are planners and are usually thinking ahead. Voila! My husband's answer was future-focused. He had assessed, prior to the manifestation of our children that they would exceed what we had done as parents.

Isn't that how God is? When He places His Gift in us to produce, He has already assessed the outcome before we deliver it. He looks ahead and determines that what's in us will be successful and perform greater works (John 14:12, NKJV). God knows that what He places in us is of Him and He cannot fail. Similar to Greg, believers need to assess the future knowing that what God is developing within them will accomplish all it was meant to do.

Most of the time, God is trying to get our faith to a place of maturity so that we will trust what He has already declared for our lives. When we can get to this point in our faith, then we will assess what God has birthed out of us from what we already knew it would be due to His prophetic word that He'd already spoken to us. As a result, we will be less concerned with comparing the appearance of our gift to others, because we will be confident when we look at our own gift, knowing that it was already declared to be unstoppable. Unstoppable, meaning that what God has purposed for it to do, it will do! In other words: its mission will be accomplished. Its mission will be accomplished not only because it is strong and mighty, but also because He who has began a good work in us will be faithful to complete it. This assurance we must have in God even before what is developing within us is manifested. This is what Greg was demonstrating! The key is that we remain faithful to Him until He has completed the process.

Finally, remember I mentioned to you that as soon as the baby is delivered, loved ones often abruptly change their focus from the new mom to the new baby. It's not their intention to be insensitive or inattentive; they are simply fascinated and in awe of the beauty, greatness, and life of this new gift. Nevertheless, at times, mom's weariness, pain, and response from giving birth can sometimes go unnoticed as a result.

The same thing happens in the Body of Christ. Once believers birth forth what God has placed inside of them, individuals can become so fascinated by the anointing, beauty, and greatness of what God has released through them (those who have just pushed out gifts), that sometimes their weariness, pain, and response to manifesting the gift goes unnoticed. For this reason, I speak to my fellow leaders in the Body of Christ and admonish you to make the necessary postpartum (after birth) assessments and examination in the lives of those that are delivering.

When assessing, don't just focus on quantity during your assessment. That's what new parents do when they are counting to make sure baby has all its fingers and toes. Focus on quality during your assessment. That's what the medical staff does when they are assessing the heart rate, activity, breathing, and so on. We are assessing the quality of life. In order to perform excellent assessments and examinations within the Body of Christ, good leadership in the Kingdom of God is essential. Meet with those that are laboring and delivering in your local church. Lovingly communicate with them to ensure that they are well. Don't get so fascinated by what they are producing in the Kingdom that you forget to assess how *they* are doing. Ask them, don't assume. Remember, those enjoying the gift, will not often think about assessing the well-being of those producing and stewarding the gifts. Many remain in awe of what was birthed recently, months ago, and even years down the road.

Many times I have to repair post-delivery injuries that my patient is not even aware that they have sustained. Why aren't they aware they sustained an injury? Because, they are not in the position to see what I see, and other times they are not in a state to feel what I see. When I discover an injury, it's because I am actively searching for it! It's necessary to prevent further complications. Not to mention, it's my job to do so! Make sure your assessments are thorough and detailed. Furthermore, what makes it easy for me to discover injuries is the willingness of my patients to allow me to do a thorough exam, despite the discomfort they may feel during these exams.

Therefore, I say to the Children of God, be willing to allow your leadership to assess you and your gift regularly. It's imperative to ensure that the purpose it was designed to accomplish is not compromised in anyway. Moreover, it is to ensure that the life of the gift is not compromised in a way that causes death to itself or to others.

About the Author

Chevelta A. Smith, D.O., is a board certified Obstetrician and Gynecologist, pastor, marriage coach, educator, and published medical author. Dr. Smith is a dynamic and powerful speaker—both medically and spiritually. She has been gifted with a phenomenal ability to parallel the medical and spiritual, in a way that is tremendously life applicable. Moreover, she is known for delivering the Word of God in a lively, non-traditional, and dramatic way, and often uses her medical knowledge to dissect God's Word. She has touched the lives of many across the nation through the broadcast ministries of "Resurrection Today, TBN, Streaming Faith, and her former radio show, *Straight Talk with Dr. Chevelta,* featured on Gospel Impact Radio during the year 2013-2014. She, along with her husband, founded B.E.D. Marriage Ministry over 15 years ago, which was later re-launched as the B.E.D. Marriage Movement in 2011. Marriages throughout the country have been revitalized, enhanced, and revived by their distinctively powerful tag-team style of teaching and counsel.

Dr. Smith worked as an Assistant Professor and the Director of the Women's Health Curriculum for the Rowan University Medical

School from 2011-2013. Her captivating and unique teaching style impacts many, both in and outside of the medical classroom and community. Over the years, Dr. Smith has become known for her lively and energetic *Spice Up Your Sex Life* workshop, which she has presented for various health and marriage conferences within the Philadelphia, Delaware, and New Jersey area. Dr. Chevelta has recently launched her brand, Raw Medicine. This platform is purposed to provide natural and spiritual healing, as well as improve the quality of individual lives by delivering a living, whole, and fresh word via videos, TV, radio, writing, and speaking engagements. She believes in inspiring individuals to discover their purpose and live authentically.

Although a native of Washington, D.C., Dr. Chevelta A. Smith currently resides and practices medicine in Pennsylvania. She continues to educate medical residents and students with excellence.

Dr. Smith has been happily married for more than two decades and has three beautiful children.

For more information on Dr. Chevelta Smith, visit her blog site, Raw Medicine, at www.rawmedicinelive.com.

You may also follow Dr. Chevelta Smith on Facebook and Twitter.

www.ingramcontent.com/pod-product-compliance
Lightning Source LLC
Chambersburg PA
CBHW021405290426
44108CB00010B/391